BUCKET

~ TO ~

GREECE

Volume 8

V.D. BUCKET

All names have been changed to spare my wife
embarrassment.

Editor: James Scraper

Proofreader: Alan Wood

Cover: German Creative

Interior Format: The Book Khaleesi

Other Books in the Bucket to Greece Series

Bucket to Greece Volume 1

Bucket to Greece Volume 2

Bucket to Greece Volume 3

Bucket to Greece Volume 4

Bucket to Greece Volume 5

Bucket to Greece Volume 6

Bucket to Greece Volume 7

Bucket to Greece Collection Vols 1-3

Bucket to Greece Collection Vols 4-6

Chapter 1

The Dirt Terminator

Y ou'll have to shift all this junk, Victor. You've got enough clobber down here to open a market stall," Barry decreed, eyeing the boxes piled up in a dark corner of the downstairs storage. I shuddered at the prospect of investigating their contents, an undoubtedly foul task that would require getting up close and personal with dusty, mosquito clogged cobwebs.

"I expect half of the stuff is Marigold's superfluous tat that she brought over from

Manchester and the other half most likely belonged to Spiros' dead uncle..."

"The one that met an untimely end by plummeting off your roof?" Barry chortled, showing no respect for the splattered corpse.

"Well, it wasn't my roof when he fell off it," I clarified, preferring to distance myself from such a messy ending.

"Well, the boxes will have to go. We want to get started on the floor tomorrow and that lot is in our way. I'll give you a hand to sort through them if you like, work out what you want to keep and what can be binned," Barry offered.

I reluctantly conceded that Barry had a point. He and Vangelis were hard at work converting our downstairs storage into a separate abode for Violet Burke. Although my mother had been on the fence about accepting my offer to live part of the year in Meli, I had managed to talk her round by turning on my persuasive charm during a recent flying visit back to England. The sole purpose of said trip had been to assist Violet Burke in moving out of the flat above the condemned chippy: suffice it to say, I had not been impressed by the depressing dwelling in a less than salubrious area that she had been allocated by the council. Quite how the housing officials could expect Violet Burke to live in harmony with the dreadful Billings woman next door was beyond me. She had been a regular at the chippy. Suffice it to say that my mother had grossly under exaggerated the toxicity of her ghastly new neighbour when she had complained about the awful woman. By now, Mrs Billings and her demands for plaice every Friday had acquired a certain infamy in my mind.

Considering the amount of work involved in transforming the downstairs storage, or the *apothiki* as we had more correctly taken to calling it, I was seriously beginning to regret the whole thing. On top of the work, I had to suffer Marigold flashing my credit card and ordering the most expensive fittings for the conversion.

"Was he very religious?" Barry asked, sifting through the contents of the most accessible box.

"Who?"

"The chap who fell off your roof?"

"It wasn't my roof when he fell off it," I reiterated, annoyed that Barry insisted on making out I lived in some kind of death trap. "And I've no idea if he was observant."

In truth, I knew little about Spiros' dead uncle

beyond his appalling taste in cheap aftershave and his propensity for dying his hair with boot polish. "Why do you ask if he was religious?"

"Well, this box is stuffed full of old icons," Barry said. "Do you want me to dump them in the bins?"

"That sounds a tad sacrilegious. Put the box to one side, Barry. I'll try to palm the icons off on Papas Andreas."

No sooner were the words out of my mouth than I regretted them. Marigold's good friend and former fellow pet food taster, Geraldine, was due to arrive for a holiday the next day with her latest chap in tow. Considering her previous unsuitable dalliance with Andreas, it may be more prudent to avoid the esteemed cleric for the foreseeable, particularly if Geraldine had any ideas of flaunting her new fellow under his nose. Sharing the news of Geraldine's impending stay with Barry, my brother-in-law responded, "Not that man-mad harpy," his words punctuated with an exaggerated eye roll.

"Now, Barry, you know how Marigold likes to remind us that Geraldine just hasn't been as lucky in love as we have. This new chap she's dragging over may well be the one."

"He must want his head examining. What's

his name?"

"I haven't got a clue. I must confess that I tend to tune out when Marigold starts bleating on about Geraldine. I do know that he analyses sexually transmitted infection samples for a living…"

"Not really the sort of thing you want in your spare bedroom," Barry sympathised. "Cynthia didn't take to Geraldine."

Before I could respond with a quip about Cynthia's green-eyed streak, Barry sent a box clattering to the ground, its contents spilling out.

"Why would anyone keep hold of a load of old *brikis* missing their handles?" Barry asked, chewing his lip in confusion. "Oh, gross, this old jar is disgustingly sticky. I think this is one for the bin."

"Not so fast," I exclaimed. "Is that what I think it is? Pass it over." Barry's find may be unpleasantly sticky but it appeared to be an old, perhaps even ancient honey jar complete with dipper. Handcrafted from olive wood, it seemed to be in mint condition if one overlooked the honey smears. I had been hankering after an authentic honey dipper and was thrilled that Barry had unearthed one of such unique appearance, complete with matching jar.

"Whilst admittedly I'm no expert, this could be quite a find after a good scrubbing."

"I prefer a squeezy bottle, myself." I winced at Barry's boorish response.

Tentatively thrusting my hands into a cardboard box, I was dazzled by a swirl of psychedelic orange. An image of our first marital home flashed before my eyes as I recalled the patterned brown shag pile paired with geometric orange drapes. Sometime Marigold's actions baffle me; I could see no logic in the madness of carting dated curtains from our first home to a house complete with wooden shutters in Greece.

As Barry delved into the contents of another box, his cheery tone turned to one of complaint. "This Christmas sweater still has the label on it. Didn't you ever wear it?"

Peering through the shuttered gloom, I recognised one of Barry's more tasteless Christmas offerings, a joke of a brightly knitted pullover featuring the slogan 'Jingle.' Whilst the caption itself may pass inspection as innocuous, it was plastered above two bells indelicately positioned where my manly nipples would be, should I be vulgar enough to don it. Before I could respond, Barry held up yet another rejected Christmas offering, a tee-shirt emblazoned with the image of a feather duster, ridiculously embellished with actual feathers. The slogan read, 'The Dirt Terminator'.

"Very droll, Barry. Why do you persist in gifting me unsuitable items of clothing that you know I will never wear?"

"It amuses me."

"Well, your luck is in. Put them to one side and I will give them to Guzim; he loves nothing more than a tasteless cast-off. You can satisfy your juvenile humour by mocking my gardener."

"It won't be the same..." Barry's words were cut short as the bottom of the box he was manhandling fell through. As he pounced on the contents with interest, I exhaled with relief, recognising my prize collection of restaurant menus dating back to the 60s and 70s. Whilst menus from more recent years were safely stashed in my home office, I had been certain that Marigold had callously chucked out my earlier collection when we'd upped-sticks to Greece. It appeared that I owed my wife a grovelling apology.

Grabbing a menu, I perused the list of dishes.

"They didn't have much imagination back in the days of pre-decimalisation. The only starters on this one are tomato juice, tomato soup or egg mayonnaise."

"Same here," Barry said, waving an egg shaped menu around, bringing back satisfying images of the Golden Egg passing their hygiene inspection with flying colours. "Tomato juice, tomato soup, or half a grapefruit. Their idea of a salad was nothing more exciting than lettuce and tomato."

I suppressed a snort; back in the 60s, Barry had spurned salad and his idea of a vegetable had been a fried potato. Nothing much changed on the vegetable aversion front until our move to Greece had introduced Barry's taste buds to a whole new world of previously despised greens, a thought borne out by his next words.

"These starters weren't very tempting. I took Cynthia out last night; we had appetisers of baked feta with honey and crispy fried aubergines. Little Ana had her first taste of mashed up cheese pie."

"It won't be too long until her teeth start coming through and she'll be able to take her first bite," I said.

Thrusting a post-decimalisation menu from

Wimpy under my nose, Barry pursed his lips and unleashed a whistle. "Five and a half pence for a cup of tea, Tina charges more than that for a single teabag these days. What on earth was a shanty salad?"

"Fried fish with a bit of iceberg," I enlightened him.

"I'm surprised so many of these menus you saved are from chains," Barry said, pulling out a menu from the Berni Inn. A wave of nostalgia washed over me.

"I proposed to Marigold over dinner in the Berni Inn in 67, it had just opened in Manchester that year," I confided.

"Did she say yes?"

"Let me give you a clue: we've been married for thirty seven years. If you recall it was only my timely intervention that prevented you from ritual humiliation at the wedding," I reminded Barry. His face turned puce, no doubt remembering that his sister had been quite set on her pimply teenage brother being a page boy until I had intervened to spare him the indignity.

"Do you remember the Berni Meringue Fountain?" Barry asked, adroitly changing the subject.

"Ice cream and fruit on a meringue, served

with cream. The fruit wasn't out of a tin," I said, reflecting fresh fruit was a bit of novelty back in the day.

"Who would have guessed that the Berni Inn was doing Greek food back in the 70s? Look at these starters, Victor; *taramasolata*, fruit juice, soup of the day and prawn cocktail."

"I do believe it was their *taramasolata* that first gave Marigold exotic ideas about holidaying in Greece," I said.

Our culinary reminisces were interrupted by the door creaking open and sunlight flooding the room.

"I might have known I'd find you two skulking in here," Marigold said in an accusatory tone. "Victor, you know that I need you to give me a hand upstairs. We want to make a good impression on Ashley."

"We aren't skulking; we are sorting through these boxes," Barry argued.

"And who on earth is Ashley?" I demanded, clueless why I should want to make a good impression on a woman that I had never heard of.

"Really, Victor. Sometimes I think that you never listen to a word that I say. Ashley is Geraldine's new chap, they'll be here tomorrow.

Surely you recall, I told you they were driving down from Athens."

"Why has Geraldine's new fellow got a girl's name?" Barry asked.

"His mother named him after Leslie Howard, apparently she had quite a thing for him," Marigold said. Barry and I stared at Marigold as though she had lost her marbles, her explanation making no sense.

"But you just said he was called Ashley," Barry pointed out.

"Yes, after Ashley Wilkes in 'Gone With the Wind.' He was played by Leslie Howard in the film but Ashley's mother didn't want to call him Leslie, she thought it may get confusing since Lesley was becoming popular as a girl's name."

"So she called him by another girl's name?" Barry said, clearly perplexed.

"Ashley was a boy's name back then. Now, I don't want the two of you teasing him about it; Geraldine did mention he can be a bit sensitive."

"What, us? Perish the thought," I said, winking at Barry.

"So, you'll make an effort to get on with him?" Marigold pressed.

"I won't be around much. I've an early start on Pegasus *methavrio*, it's the Caves of Diros trip," I said, relieved to be spared at least one day of the sexually infected chap's company even if I couldn't conjure up some excuse to be out of the way when they arrived the next day. Of course there was an outside chance that Ashley may not actually be insufferable, but his taste in women marked him down as suspect.

"Have you had any luck finding alternate work, Victor," Barry asked.

"I can't say that sticking labels on bottles in the olive oil factory really grabs me," I sighed. With the tourist season about to end, my days of repping would be put on hold until the following year. The prospect of enforced idleness held little appeal; I rather enjoyed having a part time job to keep me occupied. Nikos balked at the idea of paying me wages to chef in the taverna when he had Dina and Eleni on hand to work for nothing, and I had cunningly invented a bad back as a handy impediment to toiling in Panos' fields.

"I've told you, sell some of this junk. Is there a Greek equivalent of a car boot sale? It would keep you busy and bring in some cash," Barry suggested.

"There's hardly going to be a roaring trade in handleless *brikis*," Marigold sneered, sifting through the unboxed junk. Catching sight of the menus, she added, "Oh, for goodness sake, I thought I'd seen the last of those. I hope you intend to bin them, Victor."

"Not a chance, they have sentimental value," I defended.

"I sometimes think that you have lost the plot, Victor. You don't see me getting all sentimental about my days as a pet food taster."

"These menus aren't all related to my illustrious career as a public health inspector," I argued. "Look, here's the menu from the night I proposed to you in the Berni Inn."

"You can't expect him to bin that one, Sis. Surely you have tender memories of the moment when Victor went down on one knee?" Barry protested, taking my side as usual.

"Would that he had. Victor didn't quite manage the whole getting down on one knee..." Marigold scoffed.

"The intention was there," I interrupted. "I would have done it but for that rather suspect spillage on the carpet. I wouldn't have looked my most dapper with a damp patch on one knee. Anyway, you're a fine one to talk about carting junk to Greece. What on earth were you thinking dragging those vile orange curtains across Europe?"

"Fabric can always be repurposed…" Marigold started to argue.

"Then why do you always insist on buying new?" I countered, recalling the small fortune Marigold had dropped on new soft furnishings.

"Just take them to the bins, Victor," Marigold commanded. "And don't be all day about it, I need you to turn the mattress in the spare room. Considering his line of work, Ashley may be a bit paranoid about what he sleeps on."

Chapter 2

Tina's Tempting Proposition

Barry proved as good as his word, helping me to sort through the accumulated junk, finally persuading me that there was a bob or two to be made in the Greek equivalent of a car boot sale. When Barry offered up a spot in his own garden shed to store the miscellaneous stuff selected as having possible resale value, we duly lugged the boxes across the village square. My old menus were safely stashed in my home office along with the icons; Barry's old Christmas presents of unsuitable clothing had been put to one side to give to Guzim and we had stuffed the assorted soft furnishings into bin bags and dragged them across to the communal village bins. I felt a tad guilty that bulky bags of curtains and other assorted odds and ends were taking up valuable space reserved for household refuse. Still, I reflected, if the villagers couldn't cram all their leftovers into the overflowing public bins, it may encourage them to start taking recycling more seriously: their haphazard approach was lax to say the least.

Bidding farewell to my brother-in-law, I turned towards home, dragging my steps to delay my return in the hope of avoiding as much of the busy-work that Marigold had invented in anticipation of Geraldine's arrival. Already aching from carrying boxes, I had no desire to torment my muscles further by turning mattresses. Putting off the inevitable, I decided to call in the village shop and treat Marigold to some *halva*: the sweet confection invariably earning me brownie points in the buttering up stakes.

Crossing the village square, I chuckled at the sight of a couple of bicycles securely chained up, presuming they must belong to a pair of tourists exploring off the beaten track. With no crime in the village, the only things the locals needed to chain up were ferocious guard dogs. Observing a couple of unfamiliar Lycra clad fellows relaxing under the shade of a plane tree, I nodded in greeting, presuming they belonged to the aforesaid bicycles.

During the intense heat of summer, I had suggested to Dimitris that we conduct our language lessons under the shade of the plane trees rather than on his sun exposed, streetside doorstep. Dimitris, being a creature of habit, had rebuffed my suggestion, refusing to shift from his doorstep even when I presented the compelling argument that such a tree shaded study area had been good enough for Hippocrates to school his students in the finer points of medicine. I must confess to being unable to counter Dimitris' argument that Hippocrates would not have chosen to sit on the ground beneath a shady plane tree if comfortable chairs had been invented since I had rather sizeable gaps in my knowledge about Ancient Greek furniture. There was certainly nothing remotely comfortable about Dimitris' hard backed chairs but my learned professor friend had the final word, pointing out that his doorstep was conveniently placed for him to brew coffee in his *briki*.

Entering the shop, I inhaled the tantalizing

aroma of coffee and herbs, along with something that smelt suspiciously like damp dog. I
welcomed the relative coolness compared to
outdoors. Since no one appeared to be manning
the store, I took my time idling along the aisles,
always intrigued to spot an unfamiliar Greek
item. Picking up a packet of *moustoukoura*, I was
momentarily stumped by the description of
'Traditional Greek Must Cookies,' racking my
brain until I recalled that 'must' was something
to do with fermented grape skins. A vivid image
of Guzim stomping the grapes with his scabby
feet made me drop the cookies like a hot potato.

Doubting that Marigold had whipped up a
three-course dinner, being otherwise occupied
with mopping up dead mosquitoes and ensuring the spare bedroom linen was pristine and
crease free, I presumed the preparation of the
evening's repast would fall on my shoulders. I
hoped to find inspiration for a quick yet tasty
meal for the evening, knowing that Marigold
would have me slaving over a hot stove the next
day to knock up something to impress her
guests. I reflected that at least the presence of the
sexually infected chap would spare me from
cooking for one of the infernal dinner parties
thrown with the express intention of dangling

eligible bachelors under Geraldine's nose: her friend's coupled up state put a spanner in my wife's meddlesome matchmaking.

The sight of some plump ripe avocados sent my culinary imagination soaring. I would pile them on toasted bread drizzled with *fava*, topping the fruit with crumbled *feta* and black olives. Simple yet delicious: *aplo alla nostimo*.

Thinking our houseguests would no doubt welcome a digestif, or *peptiko*, I ambled along to the spirit selection. A bottle of mastic liqueur from Chios caught my eye, but I was once again stumped by the main ingredient of *mastichi*, having never tasted the resin derived from mastic trees. The only resin I was familiar with was the vile pine stuff that went into the popular *Retsina*, in my humble opinion a nasty wine best served as a toilet cleaner. Deciding to stick with something familiar, I added a bottle of *Metaxa* to my basket, hoping that Geraldine's new fellow wasn't discerning enough to distinguish the difference between three star and seven star brandy. Picking up the cheapest bottle of the famous Greek spirit, I couldn't fail to notice that the shelf was in desperate need of not only a good dusting but a thorough scrubbing.

"Kalispera, Kyrios Bucket." The bottle almost

slipped through my fingers when Tina greeted me: I hadn't heard her stealthy approach.

"Victor, please, no need to be so formal," I responded, relieved that at least in her formality, Tina had stuck to Bucket rather than addressing me as *Kyrios Kados*. The latter was an irritating habit some of the other villagers had adopted, supplanting my surname with the literal Greek translation of Bucket.

"I am the happy to see the you," Tina said in tentative English, invariably keen to practice her foreign language skills.

"And I you," I replied, returning her broad smile. It was always a relief when Tina served in the shop rather than her wart-faced, old hag of a mother. Despina took great delight in using her malicious tongue to spread scurrilous gossip, forcing the villagers to scope out the shop to check that the coast was clear of her toxic presence before entering. It was only Tina's pleasant personality that retained the villagers' loyalty, no mean feat considering how eye-wateringly expensive some of her prices were in comparison to the supermarket chains. Such is the cost of convenience: an extra ten cents on a roll of toilet paper is a small price to pay to avoid the three-hour round trip to town.

"I talk with the Spiros, earlier," Tina said. "He tell to me that you to look for the work."

"Indeed, my repping job is about to end for the season and I like to keep myself busy."

"I have the proposition for the you. I need the help in the shop."

Adopting a nonchalant expression, I wondered how I could wiggle my way out of this one. Nothing would induce me to work alongside Despina; the woman was pure poison. Before I could think up some plausible excuse that wouldn't offend Tina, she continued:

"*I mitera mou* must to go in the hospital in *Athina* for the new *gonato*, how to say in the English?"

"A new knee," I said, perking up at the thought that Despina would be out of the way in a hospital bed.

"Yes, the new knee. I must to be at the hospital with the *mama*. It is the very difficult, I have no the one to run the shop. The Athena can to help in the afternoon when she to finish the hair and the Kyria Kompogiannopoulou will to help if the *kysti* not play up…"

"I didn't realise she was still having problems with her bladder," I said.

"Yes, she can to work in the shop but will not

be the very help if she to spend half the time in the toilet," Tina sighed. "I need the help when I must to be at the hospital with the *mama* or I must to close the shop in the mornings. Thalia will to help after the school, she is the good girl."

"So, you have Athena working in the afternoons and Kyria Kompogiannopoulou doing the odd shift, her bladder allowing, and your niece, Thalia, working after school," I clarified.

"That is the yes. But the morning is the most important; it is the more busy time and have the deliveries. *Ti boro na kano*?" Tina threw her head backwards, clucking her tongue while holding her hands aloft to punctuate her last point, a seemingly universal Greek expression of 'what can be done?' "You have the good reputation in the village, Victor. I to trust my shop in the hand of the capable you."

"I'm flattered," I said, mulling over her offer and surveying my potentially new domain. With Despina out of the way, I imagined that manning the shop could well be interesting. It would offer a wonderful opportunity to interact with the villagers and hone my ever improving Greek language skills. There was certainly no doubt that my expertise in hygiene would come in handy since the dusty shelves were most off-putting; I could have those sorted in a jiffy.

"If you can to work when I must to be in the *Athina* hospital with the *mama*, I think for the one week, and after, when she is the home she will be the...how to say?"

"Barking orders and running you ragged," I suggested. Tina's resigned expression confirmed my theory. I imagined Despina must have driven her mad with her nagging, guilt tripping Tina into playing the role of dutiful daughter at her hospital bedside, forcing her to put her mother before her business.

"I can to pay you the five *evro* the hour but no to tell that to the, what is the word, the *antras foros*?"

"The tax man," I translated with a knowing wink.

"And not to tell the five *evro* to the Athena or the Kyria Kompogiannopoulou, because I pay to them the less," Tina tempted me. Five euros an hour was not to be sniffed it. Not only was it a superior hourly rate than repping, the job in the shop would involve nothing more than a gentle stroll across the village square rather than the taxing drive to town and back which repping entailed.

"I'd like to help you out but I still have a

couple of excursions to do for the tour company," I said. "When would you need me to start?"

"The *mama* must to be in the hospital on this Thursday...I must to be next to the bed for the week."

"That could work; I've a boat trip on Wednesday and then my final excursion next week. Cynthia may be able to find someone else to cover that one. But I couldn't just start working in here without knowing the procedure for taking deliveries...not to mention getting to grips with making the coffees that you serve outside and mastering the till."

"Can you to come in the tomorrow for me to show you how it all to work?"

"Eight in the morning," I suggested, thinking a day in the shop under Tina's tutelage should be adequate training for assuming the role of shop manager later in the week.

"Victor, I could to the kiss you," Tina gushed. Restraining herself, she insisted I take the avocados and the *halva* on the house, only accepting payment for the bottle of *Metaxa*. Bidding Tina goodbye, I mused how well things had worked out. Working in the shop would put a suitable distance between myself and

BUCKET TO GREECE (VOL. 8)

Marigold's houseguests without the need for me to come up with elaborate excuses to avoid them if they got underfoot.

Chapter 3

Guzim Anticipates a Visitor

T here you are at last, Victor. When you and Barry get together you are worse than a couple of old gossips. Only the pair of you could make a trip to the bins last the best part of a couple of hours," Marigold complained on my return.

"I made a slight diversion to buy you this," I said, depositing a kiss on her cheek and thrusting the *halva* under her nose by way of a peace offering.

"Bribing me with sweet treats just isn't going

to cut it this time, Victor. You knew that I needed your help to spruce the house up before Geraldine's arrival. I nearly did my back in turning the spare room mattress."

"Geraldine is pretty easy going. She'll be happy to take us as she finds us," I pointed out.

"Yes, but this Ashley fellow may have exactingly high standards."

"Unlikely, after all, he is walking out with Geraldine," I muttered under my breath.

"I heard that," Marigold snapped, sending a withering look in my direction.

"Well, let's hope this bottle of the finest *Metaxa* meets with his approval," I said, flashing the bottle under Marigold's nose.

"You could have sprung for the expensive stuff for once...must you always embarrass me by being such a skinflint?"

"There's no point in wasting the good stuff on Geraldine and her fellow, for all we know he may share Geraldine's atrocious habit of diluting his brandy with Fanta *lemoni*," I said, wincing at such an execrable practice. "Now, if you'll excuse me, I'm off for a refreshing shower. Once cleansed of *apothiki* grime, I will prepare a light evening meal of *avokanto se tost me fava kai feta*. I thought we could enjoy it on the roof terrace."

"There's no need to bother, Victor. Spiros invited us to join him and Sampaguita for dinner at the taverna."

"Just because the taverna is likely to be filthy is no reason to skimp on my personal hygiene," I quipped.

"I meant that you needn't bother preparing food, just as well as the combination of *fava* and avocado sounds altogether too mushy. A shower is most definitely in order; you have the rather pungent whiff of bins about you."

Unsure if Marigold was simply winding me up, I surreptitiously sniffed my clothing whilst filling her in on my fortuitous luck in landing a new job, explaining that I would be gainfully employed during Despina's hospital spell in Athens and her subsequent home recuperation.

"So, did Tina actually offer you the position of temporary shop manager or have you simply promoted yourself from the more humble role of shop assistant?" Marigold asked, sarcasm lacing her tone.

"Well, she's leaving me in charge...and since I am being paid more than both Kyria Kompogiannnopoulou and Athena, I assume that gives me seniority on the pecking scale."

"If you're expecting to boss Kyria Kompogiannopoulou about then you will need to master the art of doing it through the bathroom door. I hear that she's never out of the toilet..."

"Apparently there's a long waiting list for bladders," I explained.

"I heard that Kyria Kompogiannopoulou refused to hand over a brown envelope," Marigold said in a whisper, as though the very mention of bribery should not be spoken aloud.

"Well, maybe she'll be able to afford to stuff one now that she's doing a few shifts in the shop. Speaking of the shop and my managerial position, I do have seniority over Thalia, and she's family."

"She's still a schoolgirl, Victor. For goodness sake, don't go getting all self-important and lording it over the poor child." Marigold's exasperated words were accompanied by a look so withering that I feared I may be relegated to sleeping on the couch. A hint of a smile softened her features as she continued, "Anyway, I am absolutely delighted that you won't be joining the ranks of the unemployed. I think it's nice that you'll be able to keep yourself busy, dear. To be quite frank, I've been dreading you getting under my feet once you finish repping. And as you'll be working locally, I will have the car at my disposal. Yes, that suits me just fine."

"I'm glad it meets with your approval. I will be doing in-house training tomorrow, I start first thing. I'm afraid you will have to prepare dinner for your houseguests…"

"Oh, Victor, I was rather counting on you to rustle up something authentically Greek to impress Ashley."

"I do have a rather tasty homemade rabbit *stifado* in the freezer that you could defrost," I suggested, recalling the succulent meat which Giannis the bee man had given me in return for my luscious offering of figs.

"And what if he's got a thing about eating rabbit?" Marigold asked, having nobly overcome her own supposed aversion to eating bunnies when she'd tasted the delectable *kouneli stifado* I had prepared. I rather think it was the addition of honey, thyme and rosemary, together with a subtle smattering of cumin seeds, which gave the dish such an irresistible edge.

"Just tell him it is chicken," I countered, flouncing off for my shower.

Towelling myself off, I heard Marigold calling me, her voice imbued with a sense of panic. Recognising the guttural accent of Guzim, I hastily dressed, wondering why he was apparently pestering my wife on our doorstep: she would certainly never dream of inviting him over the threshold. Since Marigold had taken rather a dislike to the Albanian shed dweller, she much preferred it that I be the one to interact with the gardener.

Joining them on the doorstep, I noticed that Marigold resembled a deer caught in the headlights, clearly unable to comprehend a word of Guzim's enthusiastic guttural ramblings. He appeared so excited by something that he may have even reverted to his native tongue rather than speaking Greek.

"*Mila arga*, Guzim," I said, instructing him to speak slowly.

"*I Luljeta erchetai stin Ellada, i Besnik tin odigei edo me ta kounelia.*" Guzim practically belched the words at such great speed that it took me a moment to mentally translate them. It appeared that his wife Luljeta was coming to Greece: Besnik was driving her with the rabbits. Recalling that their Albanian compatriot, Besnik, was loosely related to Luljeta, my curiosity was piqued as to why the building foreman was transporting rabbits across national borders.

"What's he saying?" Marigold demanded.

My wife never has the patience to attempt to decipher Guzim's accent.

"His wife, Luljeta, is on her way to Greece," I duly informed her.

"His wife. When does he expect her?" Marigold asked with sudden interest.

"*Pote tha einai i Luljeta?*" I said, asking when she would be here.

"*Afti tin evodmada, den xero akrivos,*" Guzim replied.

"He says this week, he doesn't know exactly when," I translated for Marigold's benefit.

"Yes, I understood that. Is she coming alone or with their children?"

"*Einai i ynaika sou fernei ta paidia?*" I said, translating Marigold's question for Guzim's benefit.

"*Den borei na taxidepsei me pente paidia, menei stin Alvania me tous goneis mou.*"

I gasped at Guzim's reply, not sure whether to be more surprised that Guzim had actual parents to leave his children with or that he had five children. The last I'd heard, he had four sprogs. Admittedly, he had mentioned that his wife was pregnant again but there certainly hadn't been any birth announcement. I would hardly have been likely to miss it: Guzim had made a great song and dance over the birth of his son and heir, Fatos, named after the prime minister of his homeland.

"*Eichate alla moro, pote den eipes,*" I said. Noticing Marigold raise her eyebrows in confusion, I translated for her benefit, too caught up in the moment to wonder why she seemingly couldn't make head or tail of my Greek. "I said, I didn't know they'd had another baby, he never mentioned it."

"*Den itan simantiko, itan mono ena allo koritsi.*" Guzim leant over and spat in my garden, the gesture of contempt accompanying his derisory words that shockingly translated as, 'It wasn't important, it was only another girl.'

"Did he just say what I thought he said?" Marigold hissed.

"I'm afraid so, the birth of a girl apparently isn't worth mentioning."

"*Tessera achrista koritsia kai mono ena agori,*" Guzim shouted, shooting another glob of spit towards the garden as he ranted on about having four useless girls and only one boy. His anger abating, he fired me a toothless grin, saying maybe they would make a boy when Luljeta arrived. "*Isos kanoume ena agori otan i Luljeta ftanei edo.*"

I had no intention of translating that for Marigold's benefit. I doubted she would be able to sleep if her mind was bombarded with revolting images of Guzim engaged in hanky-panky in the slum of a shed at the bottom of our garden. Fortunately it appeared that Marigold had actual sleeping in mind, rather than other nocturnal activities, when she directed me to ask Guzim where his wife would be staying.

I will dispense with all the necessary convoluted translations thrown up by the ensuing conversation and parse the dialogue. Guzim announced that his wife would stay with him in his shed. Since it was the first time Luljeta had ever left their small village in northern Albania, he was very excited to have her visit him in Greece. Guzim was thrilled at the prospect of showing off his very own piece of Greek real estate to his wife as he was inordinately proud of owning his own stone shed. Considering his illegal status in the country when he had made the purchase, it was indeed quite a remarkable feat.

Marigold announced that we couldn't possibly allow Guzim to have a woman sleep in his hovel, declaring that it wasn't even fit for barn animals. She dropped that argument pretty sharpish when I asked if she would prefer us to put Luljeta up in our spare bedroom. Naturally that was out of the question, not only because it opened up the possibility of Guzim sneaking into our home at night, but because Geraldine and her new chap would be in there. Guzim's head swivelled between the two of us as we argued about the suitability of the shed for a member of the fairer sex, ignoring his repeated interjections of "*Ti?*" I pointed out to Marigold that the shed may well be a veritable palace compared to whatever living arrangements the Albanian couple were used to back home.

"Well, if he insists on having his poor wife stay in that hovel, I will give it a makeover," Marigold declared.

"You may find that a challenge, dear. It's an absolute flea pit in there," I warned her.

"Tell Guzim to clear out any rubbish and make the place tidy. You know what an eye I have for interior décor. I will transform his humble abode into a palace," Marigold said, getting rather carried away.

"And who's going to pay for this wondrous transformation?" I enquired.

"It needn't cost a cent. I knew those old curtains from England would come in handy for something, fabric can cover a multitude of sins if artfully arranged."

"The curtains that I dumped in the bins earlier?"

"You must retrieve them at once, Victor, before they absorb the stench of the bins. Oh, do tell Guzim what I plan to do to his shed; I can't bear to look at his hangdog expression any longer."

Knowing Guzim's tendency to cower in the face of a domineering woman, I wasn't sure how he would react to the news that Marigold intended to barge into his shed and give the place a makeover. I sensed that he would be unlikely to put up much of an argument even if he considered that Marigold was invading his privacy. I was not prepared for Guzim to prostrate himself on the ground, wrapping his arms around Marigold's shins and babbling incoherently in gratitude. Of course my poor gullible gardener had no clue what he was in for; being unfamiliar with the craze for vibrant psychedelic orange drapes that had been prevalent in England during the late sixties.

"Hop to it, Victor. They empty the bins tomorrow; you need to get all my soft furnishings back before anyone throws their rotted garbage on top of them. Tell Guzim that I expect his shed to be emptied first thing in the morning. I plan to make an early start."

With that, Marigold used the toe of her shoe to unclamp Guzim from her shins. Shooing him away, she made no effort to disguise her disdain for the pest. Guzim's high-pitched squeals of gratitude to the generous benefactor who had offered to decorate his Greek home rang in our ears as he stumbled away to make a start on clearing out his home ready for Marigold's inspection.

Chapter 4

Stuck in the Bins

I say, old chap. What on earth are you doing grubbing around by the bins? Don't tell me that you've fallen on hard times," Milton shouted over, crossing the street to join me by the stinking metal receptacles where I was mentally girding myself to overcome the repulsive task ahead.

"Do I strike you as a typical dumpster diver, Milton? I threw some old curtains away earlier and now Marigold wants them back," I explained, pinching my nose to prevent the vile smell of rotting rubbish from seeping into my nasal cavities. Staring at the untidy row of three humongous metal bins decorated with the malodorous evidence of rancid spillages, I admitted, "The problem is, I can't exactly recall which bin Barry tossed the bags in. We disposed of quite a few bags in there and it looks like other rubbish has been tossed in since."

"Well, they empty the bins tomorrow, old chap," Milton reminded me.

"If they aren't on strike."

"Well, there's only one thing for it, then. Give me a leg up and I'll have a rummage around inside them," Milton offered.

"What about your dodgy hip?" I asked a tad worried that if I took him up on his offer, he may do himself an injury. Still, rather him than me.

"Can't let a little annoyance like an artificial hip stand in the way of helping out a good friend," Milton blustered, encouraging me to cradle my hands to offer him a leg up into the nearest bin. Milton's up and over clumsy manoeuvre lacked any semblance of grace; he ended up falling head first into the bin. Fortunately, the accumulated bags of rubbish offered him a soft landing, sparing him from serious injury. Unfortunately, not all of the bags of household refuse that he landed on had been tightly secured; their contents had spilt out when they'd been lobbed in. The sound of scuffling and an outraged hiss emanated from the bin and two feral cats shot out, preceding the return of Milton to an upright position. I stifled a snort at the sight of my elderly English neighbour adorned with a slimy looking head of rotting broccoli tucked behind one ear, his hands plucking at the detritus of broken egg shells splattered in his thinning hair.

"I say, what a shocking waste, this discarded tin of cat food is still half-full. And it's the gourmet stuff too," Milton said, bending down to scoop it up. Wiping the tin clean on his shirt, he lobbed it in my direction, saying his adopted strays would be grateful as he couldn't afford to treat them to such a luxury brand. "You may be on to something here, old chap. Perhaps I should start trawling through the rubbish for a better quality of cat food."

"Well, I wouldn't feed Marigold's pampered domestics on anything that came out of those bins. It is likely to be contaminated with all manner of gross bacteria," I advised.

"Nonsense, our adopted strays have strong stomachs. If I don't feed them something tempting, they'll only be taking a trip to the bins to rummage and filch for themselves. They do it all the time."

I shuddered in horror, recalling that I had unwittingly taken a seat in Milton's cat hair ridden chairs, never for one moment suspecting that he allowed his collection of adopted ferals to ferret freely in the bins. I made a mental note to decline any future invitations to sit down in Milton's house unless he could assure me that his soft furnishing had undergone a rigorous disinfecting.

"Any sign of the curtains? There was one pair that was a very distinctive psychedelic orange. You probably remember that hideous trend from the 60s."

"Can't say I do, old chap. I was stationed in the dark depths of Africa in the 60s, lucky to see a bit of plastic sheeting, never mind curtains. I think we'd have better luck finding them if you climbed in and joined me…"

The thought was so repugnant that I shuddered, experiencing an unpleasant sensation as a wet trickle of perspiration dripped down my spine. On the other hand, Marigold would be on the warpath if I returned empty-handed now that she had a bee in her bonnet about revamping

V.D. BUCKET

Guzim's shed. An even more alarming thought struck me: if I did indeed return empty-handed, Marigold would no doubt interpret that as an invitation to go on a reckless spending spree with my credit card. I had no intention of allowing her to squander my hard earned cash on making Guzim's slum abode habitable. With great reluctance, I accepted Milton's outstretched hand, hoping the pensioner wouldn't give himself a hernia by hoisting me into the bin.

After several minutes of futile searching, I happened upon a plastic bag bursting with used toilet paper. Almost heaving in disgust, I made the risky manoeuvre of stepping into the adjacent bin, leaving Milton to forage through the abandoned kitchen waste and toilet offerings. Luckily the second bin was a better choice since most of the bin bags remained tightly sealed, though there was nothing to distinguish my own black bin bags from the identical bags of the other villagers. Tentatively poking their exteriors allowed me to get a feel of their contents; clearly a pair of curtains would create a different texture even when groped through plastic bags than a bag full of old wine bottles and plastic wrappings.

BUCKET TO GREECE (VOL. 8)

I experienced a Eureka moment as my hands closed around a bag that felt as though it contained fabric. I wasted no time in tossing it out of the bin, certain my search was at an end. Unfortunately, the bag beneath it had the same squishy texture, making me recall that Barry and I had carted three bags of old curtains, sheets and other assorted soft furnishings to the bins. I realised with a sinking heart that it wouldn't do to return the wrong bag to Marigold: whilst my mind had focused on the psychedelic orange curtains, she may be planning to knock up a new headboard out of an old candlewick bedspread or fashion drapes out of the old tartan sheets that had once graced Benjamin's bed. Safer all round to take home all the bags that Barry and I had dumped, I thought, tossing another two bin bags to the ground.

"I think I've got them all, Milton. I'm sure we only threw three bags away."

"Excellent, excellent. I've had quite a good haul, I must say. There was a good supply of cat food, not to mention an old doormat that the strays can use as a scratch pad. Here, take some of this," Milton said, offering me a square shaped bottle.

"Are you insane? I'm not drinking out of anything that has been in these bins," I asserted.

"It's not booze, it's aftershave, old chap. Not too bad, as it happens. It's not quite got the distinctive elegance of Old Spice but it should help to disguise the ghastly pong we've picked up in these bins."

"Pass it over," I conceded, tipping the contents over my head in a desperate attempt to cover the putrid aroma seeping from my body. "Now, the burning question is how are we going to get out of these bins without doing ourselves an injury? A hard landing could mean a broken ankle."

"Good point, old chap. It's a long way down and no mistake."

Having tossed three bags stuffed full of rubbish over the edge, I was now standing perilously close to the bottom of the bin, leaving its rim close to my chin. There was an added danger which I had not previously considered; the bins were the movable type with little wheelie things attached. A sudden movement could send the pair of us tearing off through the village streets at speed, with no handy brakes to stall our progress. I would never live if it down if our precarious predicament turned me into the Frank Spencer of Meli.

I stared at Milton, aghast, wondering how we could possibly extricate ourselves from the situation.

"I'm sure someone will come along sooner or later, old chap," Milton said optimistically. "And if not, the bin men will be along in the morning." His words did little to cheer me. I couldn't imagine which was worse; the humiliation of being caught stuck in the public bins or being left there to rot.

"If they aren't on strike," I reminded him.

"Well, at least we won't be bored, there's plenty or reading matter," Milton said, waving a couple of dog-eared copies of *To Vima*. "Darn and blast, I don't read Greek."

An uneasy silence settled between us as we pondered our predicament.

"I say, old chap. Isn't that Norman and Doreen?" Milton said a few minutes later, squinting at two rather blurred figures on the horizon. Before I could stop him, Milton was yelling at the top of his lungs, "Norman, help. Over here, old chap. Help."

Our British neighbours scurried over, making no effort to wipe the grimaces of shocked amusement from their faces. Firing a warning look at Norman, I told him, "Don't ask. Just get us out of here."

To their credit, Doreen and Norman both rushed to our assistance without even considering the numerous potential germs they could contract from merely touching our contaminated bodies. As they drew closer, Doreen wrinkled her nose, telling me, "I don't mean to be rude, Victor, but you may want to reconsider that aftershave."

Biting my tongue, I realised this was not the moment to vent my superiority. Grabbing hold of my upper arms, they hauled me out of the bins before turning to assist Milton, only demanding an explanation once we were firmly on solid ground.

"Marigold has decided to give Guzim's shed a makeover to make it more comfortable for his wife, who is on her way for a visit. Marigold sent me to retrieve these bags of soft furnishings which we had binned earlier." My succinct explanation would have to do: I was in no mood for idle chatter, my only wish being to burn the clothes I was wearing and stand under a scalding shower for an hour to eradicate every trace of the bins and their disgusting contents.

Nodding at Milton, I collected the three bin bags and took my leave, not bothering to acknowledge Doreen's parting comment.

"Oh, how exciting. A shed makeover, what fun. Tell Marigold that I'll be round first thing in the morning to give her a hand, we've nothing important on."

"And tell her she's welcome to a traffic cone to use as a statement décor feature, they make excellent talking pieces," Norman called after me.

I suppose that I should thank my lucky stars that it was Doreen and Norman that came to my rescue. Since they could barely string a coherent Greek sentence together between them, they would be unable to spread the word amongst the villagers about my mortifying predicament of being stuck in the bins.

Chapter 5

The Number 47 Bus

T he light was beginning to fade as I strolled home at a pace as fast as the encumbrance of three bulky bin bags allowed, eager to part ways with my stinking clothes. Not even the intoxicating scent of oleanders and bougainvillea could offer perfumed relief from the sickening stench of putrid waste emanating from my body. Barely noticing the hint of pink accenting the night sky, the last glimmer of a fading sunset, I almost came a cropper in the half-light, nearly tripping over

Cynthia's foul cat, Kouneli. The feline rapist was lurking with intent, poised to no doubt pounce and have its wicked way with some innocent feral. Pausing in my tracks, I saw an opportunity to wreak sweet revenge on the vile tomcat.

Calling out, "Here Kitty, Kitty," I dropped my bags and encouraged the scraggy cat with the mutant face to come closer before scooping it up, using it as a convenient rag to rub off some of the accumulated filth. The cat demonstrated its objection by lashing out with a claw, but I summarily dropped it before it could inflict any damage, amusing myself at the thought of the nasty taste it would encounter when it attempted it lick itself clean.

Continuing on my way, I began to regret my impulsive action. Recalling that for some inexplicable reason, little Anastasia had formed a special bond with Cynthia's vile cat, I made a mental note to call Barry as soon as I reached home. I ought to alert him to keep the cat away from the baby until he could disinfect it: the cat that is, not the baby. I doubted Cynthia would be amused if little Ana came down with fleas.

Arriving home, I was rather taken aback to notice a huge pile of junk at the bottom of my garden, desecrating the natural beauty. As I pondered the unlikely scenario that our garden had suffered an invasion of gypsies, realisation hit when a thick blanket was hurled over the fence to add to the pile. It appeared that Guzim was obeying Marigold to the letter, clearing the shed of all his infested belongings prior to her promised makeover. I was grateful that the wire enclosure prevented my chickens from wandering over and exposing themselves to all manner of contaminants. Too aware of my own repugnant stench to stop and have words with Guzim, I dropped the bin bags at the bottom of the outdoor stairs and yelled across to my gardener to give them a good hosing. Hurrying indoors, I was greeted with a volley of abuse from my ever loving wife.

"Really, Victor, what time do you call this? How long does it take to run a simple errand to the bins? It is so thoughtless of you; if we don't get a move on we'll be late meeting Spiros in the taverna."

"He's on Greek time," I snapped, stalking past her.

"Victor, what on earth is that stench? You smell as though you've been festering in a dung pile…"

"Really, darling, did you miss the subtle notes

of cheap aftershave that I poured over myself to disguise the fetid pong?"

"What? Must you talk in riddles, Victor?"

"Suffice it to say it was no picnic retrieving your precious soft furnishings from the bins. Not another word, Marigold. I am going for a shower. I intend to take my first shower in my clothes and then drop them outside the bathroom door. Kindly dispose of them."

"But that's a perfectly good shirt, Victor," Marigold objected.

"You may change your opinion once you get closer to it. I would suggest you put your Marigolds on before touching it."

"Well, really, I don't know what's got into you, Victor."

Slamming the bathroom door on the dulcet tones of my wife, I stepped into the shower fully clothed.

"Well, I hope that you're in a better mood now," Marigold grumbled when I finally emerged from the bathroom feeling refreshed, every last trace of bin grime flushed down the drain.

"You'd be in a foul mood too if you had been forced to clamber inside the bins," I retorted, having decided that I may as well come clean to my wife. It wouldn't do for her to hear about it from someone else if word of my evening's antics perchance got out.

"Inside the bins. I do hope that no one saw you, Victor. It would be most unfortunate if you got a reputation as a rag and bone man."

"I doubt that anyone would seriously mistake me for the Albert Steptoe of Meli."

"Nevertheless, it sounds quite gross…"

"Gross doesn't even begin to describe it. The bins were overflowing with loose rubbish that had spilled from the bags. I ended up knee-deep in loo roll and rotted veg."

"The bins were bound to be full; the bin men empty them tomorrow. I think you are overreacting though, telling me to throw perfectly good clothes away. They should be fine after a good boil wash."

"Don't bother, I shall burn them," I said, beginning to sense that my wife didn't fully appreciate the unhygienic ordeal I had endured.

"That's a bit drastic considering that you are always banging on about recycling. Why not just give them to Guzim?"

"Even Guzim's olfactory senses would be offended by them," I said, giving the Albanian's nose the benefit of the doubt.

BUCKET TO GREECE (VOL. 8)

My mood had improved considerably by the time we left the house, the prospect of an evening in the company of Spiros being just the tonic I needed. Guzim was lurking at the bottom of the stairs as we left, dutifully hosing off the bin bags. He appeared to be doing an excellent job, the beam of my torch reflecting the shine of the newly pristine plastic.

"*Pou pas?*" Guzim enquired where we were going.

"Don't you dare tell him," Marigold hissed, her hackles rising at the prospect that I may impulsively invite Guzim to join us as I had done after Apostolos' name day party.

"*Pame yia mia volta.*" Playing it safe, I told Guzim we were off for a walk.

"It's not that I have a problem with mixing with the help per se, not like Sherry does," Marigold said in defence of her standoffishness towards Guzim as we strolled towards the taverna, her arm tucked in mine. "I just have a problem mixing with Guzim."

"Understandable, dear. I do realise he can be a tad off-putting."

"Can you imagine what his wife must be like?" Marigold shuddered. "What sort of woman would settle for a shabby toothless husband who leaves her permanently pregnant whilst he's away in another country?"

"I must confess to finding the prospect of meeting Guzim's wife quite intriguing," I said, imagining a downtrodden, washed out woman without a tooth in her head. Recalling a conversation I'd had with Guzim, I told Marigold, "It was an arranged marriage, an odd concept in this day and age. Imagine having no say over who one ends up with as a life partner."

"It doesn't bear thinking about," Marigold agreed. "Just think of the horror of ending up tied to a boorish oik like Harold. Just the thought of it makes me realise how lucky I was to bang heads with you over that galvanised bucket in B&Q."

"I was the lucky one," I assured her.

A breeze rustled through the village lanes, heralding the beginning of somewhat cooler evenings, a welcome prospect after the suffocating heat of summer. Something shot across our path in a blur of fur. Marigold hesitated beside me, pausing momentarily until she continued her steps with a tinkling laugh. "That scared me for a moment, but it was only Cynthia's vile cat. I wonder what made it turn on its heels so quickly."

I didn't bother to enlighten my wife about my hunch that my earlier encounter with the repugnant moggie may have convinced the beastly creature to keep its distance from me in future, but I was inwardly delighted by the result. I was fed up of forever sweeping the predatory feline intruder out of our house, leaving Marigold fussing over her pampered imported cats: they were invariably thrown into panic mode by Kouneli's unwanted presence. Even Pickles was discerning enough to harbour no liking for the tomcat that had spawned him.

Reaching the taverna, I was surprised to find the outdoor seating area bereft of the usual mismatched collection of tables and chairs. Their abrupt removal was a cue that Nikos had decided that summer was officially over; in his mind, even though it was only September, it was now winter. Logically, since it was supposedly winter, all dining would henceforth take place indoors. In truth, Nikos loathed the additional work that serving customers outside entailed, forcing him to walk an additional few steps to collect the wine from the indoor fridge. He much preferred to man the outdoor grill without an audience and captive indoor diners saved Dina the bother of sweeping up fallen leaves and bugs. Dina demonstrated the same lack of enthusiasm for pushing a broom as she did for slopping a mop.

Spiros and Sampaguita had already bagged a table for the four of us but they were so engrossed gazing into one another's eyes in a romantic fashion that our arrival didn't even register. Leaving Marigold to break up the love birds, I headed directly to the kitchen to greet Dina. Before I had chance to sweep my favourite Greek lady off her feet and swing her around in what was our customary wont, Dina warned me off, telling me not to touch her. A tad confused by her unfriendly reception, Dina's unnatural reaction only began to make sense when she cried out that she wasn't hugging me after I'd been in the bins. To put the icing on the cake, she chided me for even daring to enter her kitchen, saying as an ex-public health inspector, I ought to know better. Although my first instinct was to assure her that I had been thoroughly decontaminated, I was more concerned how word had got out about my embarrassing antics.

"*Pos ixeres oti imoun stous kadous*?" I asked, demanding to know how she knew I'd been in the bins.

"*Oloi gnorizoun. Einai i syzitisi tou choriou,*"

she retorted, telling me everyone knew, it was the talk of the village.

"I knew I shouldn't have trusted that blasted Norman to keep his mouth shut," I complained as I joined Marigold and the others after flouncing out of Dina's domain.

"What on earth are you on about, dear?" Marigold said, blithely continuing without allowing me to answer. "Doreen telephoned while you were in the shower and said that they ran into you. She said that you told them about the makeover I'm planning to give Guzim's shed. Actually, I'm glad that you told them. Doreen has volunteered to help, a blessing really as she is quite skilled at repurposing bits of old fabric. You should see what she can do with a coat hanger."

"The mind boggles," I muttered in a noncommittal fashion, thinking that perchance I had misjudged Doreen and Norman by jumping to the conclusion that they had been the blabbermouths responsible for muddying my good name. It may well have been Milton that had spread the word about our trash safari: he has a tendency to be far too loose-lipped for my liking.

Spiros raised his bushy eyebrows at me in a

knowing way, clearly working himself up to having a laugh at my expense. Before he had chance to utter a witty quip about rubbish, Sampaguita saved the day by asking me how my mother was. For some unaccountable reason, Sampaguita appeared inordinately fond of Violet Burke.

"I have not seen you since you returned from England, Mr Bucket," Sampaguita reminded me. "How was your trip?"

"Victor, please. It was just a flying visit..."

"He go by the aeroplane," Spiros smugly explained.

"I used the term flying visit to refer to the fact that my time away was short rather than to reference my mode of transport," I explained to Spiros since he had failed to grasp the idiom. "The sole purpose of my trip was to help my mother to move from her flat above the chippy into her new council accommodation."

"It must have been a sad day for Violet," Sampaguita said sympathetically.

"Indeed, there's no denying it was a wrench for the old girl. She'd hoped to spend her last days in her home above the chip shop, it was quite an ordeal being forced to move," I said.

The conversation was interrupted by Dina

descending on our table with a basket of bread and a bottle of olive oil. Since there was no sign of Nikos, it also fell on Dina's shoulders to fetch the wine. Unlike her husband, Dina took the time to decant the *spitiko* from a five kilo plastic bottle, serving us with a kilo of the stuff in a glass *kanata*. As Spiros busied himself pouring the wine, my thoughts drifted back to my short visit to Warrington to assist Violet Burke with her recent house removal, an occasion that was lightened by the presence of Benjamin, my son having turned up to lend a hand to his granny.

With all her belongings packed, the flat above the chippy looked decidedly shabby and forlorn. An almost palatable sense that the very building was aware it was condemned hung in the air, as oppressively pervasive as the ever prevalent age-old smell of chip fat.

"It's the end of an era, boys," Violet Burke sighed, visibly fighting back the gulp in her throat as she took a last wistful look around her home. Aware that this must be a heart-rending moment for my mother, I admired her quiet dignity in maintaining a stiff upper lip.

"How long have you lived here, Granny?" Benjamin asked.

"It must be getting on for nigh twenty years,

give or take," Violet Burke replied. "I was in a bit of a bind after all that bad business came out about Arthur. I had to move out; it was a blasted nuisance the way the Old Bill kept turning up on my doorstep. It wasn't as though I'd a clue what the smarmy bugger had been up to. Like I told them, he'd likely have cleared out my Post Office account too if I'd had more than two farthings to rub together."

As I exchanged a perplexed glance with my son, Benjamin shrugged, indicating he was equally clueless to who this Arthur chap was or what he'd been up to.

"It was Dot that told me about the job going in the chippy. Gloria, she owned it back in the day, said I could have the flat along with the job. I was that glad to get away. I tell you, if Arthur hadn't have come a cropper falling under the wheels of the number 47, I'd have shoved him under the next bus that came along myself.

"You've lost me, Granny. Who was Arthur?" Benjamin asked.

"Arthur Burke, my fourth husband. Mind you, I'd never have wed him if I knew what his game was. He was a charmer all right, had more of the gift of the gab than even that phoney, limping reprobate, Vic. You'd think I'd have had more sense than to fall for it but, I have to give it to him, Arthur had perfected his con."

"I'm afraid you've rather lost us, Mother," I said, beginning to wish we'd never opened this latest can of worms.

Sighing heavily, Violet Burke turned her back on us. Gazing out of the window, she spoke in a steady voice devoid of emotion.

"After Lionel ran off with that trollop he got pregnant in the Odeon, I swore I was having nothing more to do with men. Nowt but trouble they are, you two excepted of course; you're good lads. Anyway, I was middling along, managing to get by on the wages my cleaning jobs brought in, until that ogre of a landlord went and put my rent up. To make ends meet, I had to take on a couple of shifts down the pub; that's where I met Arthur. He was that persistent, hardly surprising 'cos I was still a looker even in my 50s."

"I'm sure you were," Benjamin said, mouthing at me to join in his flattery.

"Indeed, you are still a striking woman today," I concurred. There was certainly no doubt that Violet Burke was no shrinking violet and would stand out in any crowd.

"Arthur stood out; always nicely dressed in

a suit and tie. We didn't see many of those down the pub. Still, I should have had more sense than to let myself be taken in by his charm...especially with him being a good ten years younger. Not that he twigged of course, what with me lying about my age."

"But you married him," I prompted.

"Aye, I did. I thought having a fellow to pay the rent would make life easier. Right from the off, he insisted I chuck in the job at the pub and knock the cleaning on the head, saying as the man of the house it was his duty to support me. I can't say it suited me having idle time on my hands, you know how I like to keep busy. As well as being idle, I was bored silly. Once we were wed, Arthur was never at home, always off on the road selling life insurance, or so he said. He'd be off for days at a time and then try to butter me up with fancy jewellery even though I've never been one for trinkets."

Beginning to suspect where this was going, I braced myself to hear that my mother had taken up with a common thief who plied her with stolen goods. The same thought must have been running through Benjamin's mind. "Were you taken in by a thief, Granny?"

"Aye, I was that, lad, but not any old common thief. No, Arthur had to go one better. It turned out he was a serial bigamist, taking up with women and then skedaddling with their jewellery once he'd emptied their bank accounts. Course he didn't get round to marrying all of them, he managed to con most of them before going through with the wedding."

"I'm a tad confused, Mother," I admitted. "You were obviously broke so why would a serial conman marry you for your money?"

"He didn't, you daft lad. The soppy apeth married me because he fell in love. It was all the other women he was playing, plying me with their jewellery, well the stuff he didn't fence. I was that mortified when I found out, I handed their trinkets back quick sharp and no mistake."

I wondered if my mother was simply deluding herself that Arthur had loved her, but then I considered her state of penury hardly made her a likely target for a gold digging Casanova.

"When Arthur went and pulled a disappearing act just six months after we wed, I was left in a right pickle and no mistake. Since I still had the rent to pay, but no job, I tried to pawn a bit of the jewellery he'd given me. That was when I nearly went and got myself arrested and the whole sorry tale came out."

V.D. BUCKET

"What happened?" I asked.

"The pawn shop called the cops 'cos one of the expensive rings that I was pawning had been reported missing by one of Arthur's lady friends. Of course I was gobsmacked to hear that he'd turned playing around into a full time job; turned out he'd never sold insurance in his life. And then I was thrown for a loop when the police told me that Arthur hadn't done a disappearing act: he was dead."

"Run over by a bus," Benjamin prompted since Violet Burke seemed off in a world of own.

"Aye, he'd been dead for weeks. One of the other women he'd wooed and cheated recognised him on the high street. He tried to do a runner to avoid her and landed up under the wheels of the number 47. Can you imagine, the daft cow only went and sobbed over his mangled body even though he'd cleared out her savings? When word got out, a few of his other women clubbed together to bury him, sobbing at his graveside they were. You couldn't credit it but they still loved him. I didn't waste any tears on him once I found out what he'd been up to. Good riddance to bad rubbish, I say."

"So if Arthur married some of these other women he targeted for their money…"

"And he didn't bother getting around to divorcing them," Benjamin interrupted me.

"It made him a bigamist," I finished. "Mother, have you considered that means that your marriage to Arthur wasn't strictly legal and you aren't actually a Burke?"

"Well I took the bugger's name and I'm keeping it, it's a damn sight better than the last one I was lumbered with," Violet Burke chuckled. Seeing our questioning expressions, she added, "Before I married Arthur, I was Violet Blumenkrantz."

"Does that mean that I have Jewish blood, Granny? I've always fancied an exotic lineage."

"No, lad, there's nothing exotic in your family tree. Blumenkrantz came from my third husband, Lionel. I never took to the name; it was too much like the Jewish version of Bloom."

"Why didn't you just revert to your maiden name," I asked.

"I never had any luck being a Bloom and I didn't fancy keeping the name of the family that disowned me."

"Well, we'll never disown you, Granny, you're a keeper," Benjamin gushed, embracing his grandmother with genuine fondness.

Chapter 6

Living in Sin

Victor, you're off with the fairies. Sampaguita was asking about your mother." The kick to my shin that accompanied Marigold's words snapped me out of my reverie.

"Mother is looking forward to spending a few months in Greece once the *apothiki* conversion is complete," I revealed.

"I am glad that she will be spending more time in Meli. I very much enjoy her excellent company," Sampaguita said with nary a trace of sarcasm. "I like listening to her tales; she has certainly led an interesting life."

"I doubt you've heard the half of it," I said, Violet Burke's latest revelations about her apparent marriage to a con artist bigamist still fresh in my mind.

"You aren't the only one who is keen for Violet to return," Marigold added. "Panos is rather taken with her."

"There you go again with your meddlesome matchmaking, I'm sure the romance you imagine is all in your head," I scolded my wife.

"Nonsense, Victor. Mark my words; they'll be walking out as a couple in no time at all," Marigold insisted. "Speaking of romance, have you two named the day yet?"

A blush suffused Sampaguita's features. As she nervously twirled the diamond engagement ring on her finger, it reflected the yellow light from the buzzing fluorescent tube dominating the smoke blackened, orange ceiling. Spiros had recently plucked up the nerve to pop the question. Fearing rejection, the poor fellow had been a bag of nerves. Knowing that I had tried and tested experience on my side, having successfully convinced Marigold to marry me, Spiros naturally sought my advice. I assured him he couldn't go wrong if he went down the romantic dinner route, sadly aware he may not be able to replicate the ambiance of my own Berni Inn moment. To Spiros' amazement, his beloved had accepted his marriage proposal. Unfortunately, she was decidedly less keen to accept his repeated proposals that they live together prior to the big day.

"No, the Sampaguita want the children at the wedding. It is not the easy to arrange the visa and the time when they can to come," Spiros said.

"And it is so expensive for them to travel," Sampaguita sighed.

"I tell to you to let me to buy the tickets," Spiros said. "The Sampaguita not allow me to pay..."

"It is too much Spiro; you have done so much for me already. I know your business is slow this year," Sampaguita insisted with stubborn pride. She made a valid, yet awkward point. Whilst it was good news all round that the number of local deaths was down, it wasn't such good news where Spiros' coffers were concerned. Most likely, he would do a better trade over the winter.

"Then if we must to wait, move in with the

me," Spiros pleaded.

"People will say terrible things about me if we live together before we are married," Sampaguita protested, blushing furiously. Spiros' head slumped on the table in a dejected fashion, frustrated in his every attempt to make his fragrant Filipana flower truly his.

"Sampaguita, does your reluctance to move in with Spiros before you are married stem from cultural norms?" Marigold asked solicitously.

"Yes, it is against my Catholic religion to live in sin," Sampaguita confided.

"You must to convert to the Greek Orthodox. Everyone know the Papas Andreas was to meeting the English friend of the Marigold and he not to excommunicate the himself," Spiros said.

"Perhaps Sampaguita holds her religious values more highly than you and Andreas do," Marigold chided Spiros.

Sampaguita blushed even more furiously as she admitted in a low voice, "It is not so much the religion. I spend some nights with Spiros but I must sneak away before first light, before the neighbour is up. I think some of the more elderly villagers would disapprove."

"Nonsense, I'm not exactly a spring chicken

yet I say live and let live," I chimed in. "Of course we are familiar with the twitching curtain mentality, our son Benjamin's lifestyle sometimes attracts unkind comments."

"The Benjamin is the out and proud," Spiros told Sampaguita.

"He lives with his life partner, Adam…"

"We the Greeks invent the homosexuality," Spiros interrupted; keen to ensure he wasn't lumped in with the twitching curtain brigade.

Marigold took the younger woman's hand and gave it a squeeze, assuring her, "You must follow your heart and not worry about the meddlesome gossips in the village."

"It is hard for me, Marigold. As a foreigner in the village, I don't fit in as easily as you do. I feel I must be more careful to conform," Sampaguita sighed.

"Nonsense, don't forget that me and Marigold are foreigners too…and your Greek is much better than ours," I asserted.

"Oh, Victor, must you be so dense? Sampaguita feels she stands out as a non-European. We are incredibly lucky in the way that the villagers have accepted us but look at the way they treat Guzim as an outsider," Marigold said, oblivious to the irony of her words.

I considered that pretty rich coming from Marigold since she was the one who held Guzim at arm's length. At least I made an effort, donating my old clothes to the gardening pest and inviting him to join me in the taverna; well, on one occasion at least.

"It is not so easy for me to fit in, I am from the more distant culture and have the different appearance," Sampaguita insisted. "I overheard harsh words in the shop; they say that I am only marrying Spiros for his money."

"You can't go taking any notice of anything that wart-faced old hag, Despina, says. I take it that it was Despina you heard gossiping," I guessed.

"Yes, it was. Even though her words were not true, it upset me greatly to think people could say such a cruel thing." As if to emphasise her point a couple of tears flowed freely down Sampaguita's face.

"Let me to put my hands round the neck of the *aschimi palia agelada*," Spiros cried, using the Greek for ugly old cow as he rose from his chair, his hands shaping by gesture his threat of strangulation.

"Sit down, Spiro," I instructed, pushing him back in his seat. "Despina will be out of action for the next few weeks, she's going in hospital for a new knee."

"And you mustn't pay any mind to any of the vitriol that comes out of Despina's mouth, she's nothing but a bitter and nasty woman," Marigold said. "Why, she had me all riled up by insinuating that Victor was cheating on me with another woman..."

"Victor," Sampaguita giggled, clearly finding the very notion utterly preposterous.

"Despina makes it her business to say terrible things about everyone. You just have to ignore her, though it's easier said than done," I advised. "Believe me; we have all suffered abuse at the hand of her vicious tongue."

"Remember those rumours she started about Litsa causing marital strife," Marigold added.

"The gentle old lady with the walking stick. She is so kind, she always takes the time to chat with me," Sampaguita said.

"And she spread that dreadful rumour that I had killed Panos' dog," Marigold reminded me.

"Well, you lucked out with that one not being true, it was a close call," I snorted. "But it was extremely rude of Despina to refer to you as a stupid English woman."

Looking around to make sure that no one was eavesdropping, Marigold hissed, "And do you recall that scurrilous gossip that Despina started about Milton visiting a brothel?"

"Quite outrageous. The notion that Milton could afford to pay for the services of prostitutes is patently ridiculous, he can barely afford to buy cat food," I pointed out.

My quip must have amused Sampaguita since I was rewarded by a delightful smile transforming her face. "I must go and wash these tears away," she said, excusing herself.

The moment that Sampaguita was out of earshot, Spiros grabbed Marigold's arm, urging her to please speak to his darling fiancée.

"Marigold, the Sampaguita listen to you. Please to try to persuade the Sampaguita to move in with the me. When she return from the Philippine, I tell her to live in the house of the dead Uncle Leo when she come back to the Meli, but I must to sell it. I must to pay the tax. I could get the good price, it have the air conditioning."

"I'll do my best, Spiro," Marigold promised. "Just don't go getting it into your head that Sampaguita is reluctant to move in with you because she doesn't love you. She loves you dearly but it is hard for her to defy the norms of her culture."

"Marigold is right but Sampaguita's not exactly some blushing virgin who must live like a nun. I seem to recall that she has three children," I said.

"The Jasmine, the Joy and the Jayson," Spiros said, struggling with the pronunciation of the unfamiliar J. "When I to sell the house of the Leo, I can to pay for the big wedding and the ticket for the children. Maybe, we to go to the Philippine for the honeymoon."

Our conversation was interrupted by the arrival of a couple of foreign strangers, intrepid souls indeed to brave the quizzical stares fired in their direction by the curious locals. Sensing their unease at the rather frosty reception, I greeted them with a smile and a welcoming, "*Kalispera*."

Approaching me, one of the two youngish men said in slow and precise English, "Do you speak English?" having clearly jumped to the erroneous assumption that I was Greek, an easy mistake to make considering my mastery in pronouncing the Greek word for good evening so authentically. His own accent gave away his nationality as Scottish.

"Indeed, I speak English," I assured him.

"That's a relief. We were wondering if you know of any tourist accommodation in this village. We were just passing through and became rather taken with the place."

"I'm afraid there's no one with any rooms to rent. It's a bit off the beaten track," I said, thinking what a lost opportunity. I could have made a bob or two from these tourists if the *apothiki* conversion was finished and if I could talk Marigold round into letting me rent it out when my mother wasn't in situ.

"Oh, shame. It's got real character. Is the food good here?"

"The best you'll find for miles," I assured them

"*To mono fagito yia chilometra,*" Spiros chortled, laughing at his own little quip that it was the only food for kilometres.

"I'm sure I've seen those two young men before but I'm at a loss to place them," I whispered to Marigold as they claimed a table at the far side of the room. I watched in mild amusement as Dina rushed over to them, slapping a basket of bread and a large bowl of salad on their table, asking, "*Ti pineis?*"

Seeing their confusion, I called over, "She asked what you're drinking. She has wine, beer, or Fanta."

"Beer, please," they responded just as Nikos finally put in an appearance, telling the young men, "The wine is the best *spitiko*, homemade, not the inferior shop bought rubbish. The beer, he is nothing to do with me. I make the bread and the olive oil, I make the cheese. I grow the salad and kill the animal for the grill. The beer and the water, he nothing to do with me."

Listening to Nikos' polished spiel, I wondered how many times I'd heard it over the course of the previous two years. Still, it was no matter: it never got old.

The young men duly laughed on cue, saying, "Forget the beer, we'll have the wine as it's homemade. And do you have a menu?"

"What you to want with the menu? You eat the bread, you eat the cheese, you eat the *salata*. The today, I kill the chickens for the grill."

"Sounds wonderful," the new arrivals said, clearly won over by Nikos' unique brand of hospitality.

Turning to me, Nikos bellowed, "Victor," before practically crushing my ribs as he manhandled me in a suffocating embrace. "Why you not to tell me you are the down and out on the luck? When you ask for the work in the kitchen,

I not to know you are the desperate."

"I'm not desperate, Niko," I asserted. "I was just looking for some work to keep me busy once the repping season finishes."

"Oh, Victor, why you to stand on your proud instead of admitting the time is hard?" Nikos argued. "Tonight the dinner is on the me. You no pay, I insist. I cannot to have my good friend going through the bins for the food scrap. I could not to believe it of you, Victor, you, with the hygiene obsess, you who to lecture me on the swill. To think you are the reduce to the go in the bin."

"You really have got the wrong end of the stick, Niko," I protested, inwardly cursing who-ever had gossiped about me being stuck in the bins. "I'm not having a hard time, really. I threw something away in error and had to retrieve it before the bin men come in the morning."

"Well, the dinner is on me the tonight. You too, Spiro, it must be the difficult time for you with no the body dying. I put the extra chicken on the grill," Nikos called out before striding out to his grill.

I was less than amused to notice that the two Scottish strangers had eagerly lapped up every word of this exchange, no doubt coming to the erroneous assumption that I was some kind of down-and-out dumpster diver.

"Sean's very big on recycling if you want some tips," one of the men called over. Receiving one of the withering looks which I had perfected after years of being married to Marigold, the recycling chap reddened, realising that he had overstepped the mark.

"I did not think you were the down on the luck when I to hear you to go in the bins. I know you to have the new job in the shop," Spiros said as Sampaguita re-joined us, her face freshly scrubbed clean of tears.

"Victor is the new temporary manager," Marigold giggled. "We'll have to watch that the power doesn't go to his head."

"I think Mr Bucket will charm the customers," Sampaguita said with genuine warmth in her voice.

"Victor, please," I corrected. "I certainly can't do a worse job than Despina. Anyway, how did you hear the news so quickly, Spiro? Tina only offered me the position late this afternoon."

"Who you to think recommend the you? The Tina was getting the desperate. The horrible Despina make her the guilt to go to the hospital.

Tina hope the brother would to go with the mother but he say it not the manly, it is the woman work to sit by the bed."

"Is her brother Thalia's father?" Marigold asked.

"Yes. He say he do the duty by sending the daughter to work in the shop."

"That's so typical, it's always the women that get lumbered with looking after cantankerous relatives," Marigold said.

"Now to be fair, I do more than my share when Violet Burke visits," I quipped. "And I always offered to help with the search when your Aunty Beryl went on the missing list."

"Aunty Beryl was the one that had Alzheimer's like Spiros' Uncle Leo," Sampaguita recalled.

"Oh, what a sweetheart you are to remember that," Marigold said, clearly touched.

Nikos returned carrying an enormous aromatic platter of chicken wings, the lightly charred skin glistening with lemon juice and sea salt. Dina was hot on his tail, placing a huge plate of her famous chips on our table. Our conversation died down as we tucked into the delicious food, thoroughly enjoying the simple yet excellent fare.

Telling us that she would be looking after Anastasia the next day whilst Cynthia was working in the tour office, Sampaguita suggested Marigold pop over to Barry's house to visit her adorable baby niece and share a cup of Fukien tea.

"Oh, I'd love to but I've rather committed myself to giving Guzim's shed a makeover. I think it will keep me busy all day."

Marigold's reply was met with quizzical looks from our friends.

"I think you not to stand the Guzim. How he to get you to put the lipstick on the shed?" Spiros blurted in puzzlement.

"Not makeup, a makeover. Marigold has volunteered to give the shed a bit of a facelift," I explained.

"So the facelift want the lipstick, yes..."

"A makeover is a new look. I will achieve it by decorating the shed with new bedding and curtains, perhaps a quick lick of paint," Marigold said. "The place is far too much of a hovel for a woman to stay in."

"The Guzim have the woman," Spiros snorted incredulously.

"Not a woman as such. His wife Luljeta is coming from Albania to visit him," I said.

"The wife of the Guzim is not the woman?" Spiros questioned, clearly beyond confused.

"Of course she's a woman, she bore him five children. I meant he hasn't found himself a new woman round here," I clarified.

"We can't begin to imagine what his wife is like," Marigold chuckled.

"She must be the ugly to marry the Guzim," Spiros speculated.

"I shouldn't imagine she'll be an oil painting," Marigold concurred.

"I'm guessing toothless and shabby," I said.

"How can you all speak so unkindly of a woman you have never met? It must be so hard for her to be separated from her husband when he is forced to seek work in a foreign country to put food on the table," Sampaguita said in a soft voice that put us to shame. The three of us shuffled nervously in our seats, embarrassed to have been so tactless. Sampaguita clearly drew parallels between the circumstances that forced both her and Guzim to leave their children and work abroad.

"Well, when we first met Guzim, he spent all his money on Amstel," Marigold said.

"To be fair, he knocked that on the head after the birth of his son and heir, Fatos," I pointed out.

Spiros adopted a pensive expression. "It is not the easy for the Guzim wife to come, she not to have the legal paper."

"I don't know anything about that," I said. "I only know that Guzim told us that Besnik is driving her down from Albania, you know Besnik the building foreman? Apparently he's transporting some rabbits."

"I not to like the sound of that," Spiros said, his face etched with worry.

"What, rabbits?"

"The Besnik. Lately, I to hear the worrying rumour about the Besnik." Spiros' head swivelled round as he gave the taverna a none too stealthy once-over. Seemingly satisfied that no one was prying on our conversation, he lowered his voice and leaned in close. "I to hear the Besnik may have got the tied up with some leafy characters."

"Leafy characters, that makes no sense, Spiro," I said, a tad baffled by his choice of terminology. "Do you mean shady?"

"Yes, the shady, the fishy. I to think the slippery…"

"I gather you mean disreputable types," I hissed, thinking that Spiros' use of synonyms had certainly improved since he was reunited with Sampaguita. Hopefully her excellent English would rub off on his English grammar once they were married.

"I think you to know what I to mean, Victor. The *Alvaniki mafia* have the long arm."

"Surely you can't think that Guzim's wife is mixed up with a bunch of ruthless gangsters," I hissed.

"I to think if she to come to Greece with the Besnik, it is the risky," Spiros said, his voice deadly serious.

Momentarily unnerved, I dismissed my friend's concern as nothing more than a product of his overheated imagination, telling Spiros, "It is barely credible to suppose that foreign criminals would have the likes of Guzim or his wife on their radar or have anything to do with rabbits. The whole thing is too absurd for words."

"That reminds me," Marigold said. "Don't let me forget to take the rabbit *stifado* out of the freezer in the morning."

Chapter 7

Dragging Shower Curtains to Greece

I t was a shock to the old system to wake up to an empty space beside me in the bed: it was decidedly uncharacteristic of Marigold to be up with the lark. Remembering that I was due to undergo retail training prior to my new position in the village shop, I supposed that my wife must be preparing me a special breakfast, perchance even pushing the boat out with bacon and eggs. Such a cardiac inducing treat was banned except for special occasions. I expect Marigold considered my landing a new job at more than pittance level wages worth celebrating with a tasty fry-up.

Preferring to sip my first cup of coffee in solitary peace, I girded myself to make small talk over the cafetiere, only to be pleasantly surprised to find no sign of my wife. It didn't take long for it to dawn on me that her absence meant I would be deprived of the imagined breakfast bacon I had been mentally salivating over. I presumed Marigold must have got herself in a bit of a tizzy anticipating the arrival of Geraldine and that sexually infected chap she was dragging along on holiday.

No doubt Marigold would be scrutinising our home in case she had missed mopping up the odd cat hair or dead mosquito, having a tendency to let my exacting standards rather slip between houseguests. I rather suspected such a slap dash approach may be a cunning ploy on her part, to guilt me into buying her a much coveted Roomba or engaging a cleaner. I had no intention of allowing myself to be manipulated by such a transparent ruse.

Brewing my coffee, I was mobbed in an unruly fashion by the pampered imported domestics. Despite Marigold's early rise, she hadn't bothered to feed Catastrophe and Clawsome.

V.D. BUCKET

The unpleasant task of spooning out jellied cat food with a disgusting aroma had rather fallen on my shoulders due to my habit of always being first up. Recalling Milton's disgusting intention of feeding his own houseful of strays with leftovers from the bins, I spoiled Pickles by sharing my breakfast of scrambled eggs and avocado with the playful feline: the food was going begging since Marigold had still failed to materialise by the time I served up the early morning meal.

As I enjoyed a second coffee, the dulcet tones of my wife drifted up from the garden. Wandering outside to join her, I spotted Marigold over by the shed, shouting instructions in grammatically mangled Greek at a cowering Guzim. Unbelievably, considering the hour, Marigold's trusty sidekick, Doreen, was already with her, egging her on. It seemed that the prospect of making over the hovel of a shed had fired the two women up; they appeared brimful of energy. Guzim shuffled uncomfortably, his hangdog expression making it clear he was desperate to escape and leave them to it. There was to be no escape though until the Albanian shed dweller snapped to and complied with Marigold's orders to bag up whatever disgusting rags he had been sleeping on.

"*I ynaika sou tha thelei nea sentonia sto krevati.*" Marigold hectored Guzim in a badgering tone, telling him that his wife would like new sheets on the bed. Turning to me, she added, "Can you believe he expected his poor downtrodden wife to sleep on a pile of mouldering blankets under a washing line full of dripping socks?"

Chucking his random assortment of scruffy stained bedding into a bin bag, Guzim's hangdog dejection was replaced by one of grovelling gratitude. The potential shed transformation left him as excited as a rescued puppy that has just realised that his new owner isn't about to give him a good kicking. No doubt, Guzim couldn't believe his stroke of good luck to be having his shed made over by such a renowned arbiter of good taste as my wife. I hoped that Marigold wouldn't go overboard transforming the shed into a romantic love nest: there was no guarantee that Guzim's nocturnal antics would result in a second boy.

Having thrown his rags into a bin bag as instructed, Guzim appeared a tad confused what to do with said bag, tentatively offering it to my wife. Reluctant to touch it, Marigold asked me,

"What does he usually do with his washing?" Guzim stood around like a spare part, his head swivelling between us, muttering, "*Ti?*"

Ignoring the Albanian, I told my wife, "There's no point translating for Guzim's benefit. I've been in his shed and I doubt his bedding has ever been washed. I expect a good fumigating is more in order."

"Do tell him to clear off, Victor, he's just getting underfoot. I will sort everything here and make his shed look inviting: Guzim is clearly clueless," Marigold said, making impatient shooing gestures towards my gardener.

"Clueless or not he managed to get his wife pregnant five times without resorting to clean sheets or a romantic setting. There's no need to go overboard and make it too fancy," I advised as Guzim scuttled away towards his moped clutching a bulging carrier bag of chicken droppings. "Drat, I clean forgot to give him that pile of new clothes."

"Really, Victor. There's no need to start buying him new clothes on top of the wages you already lavish on him. Don't fall for his pathetic pleas of poverty, remember he is a master of manipulation," Marigold objected. "The truth could soon be out whether his wife does indeed eat all his money."

"If she's nothing but skin and bones, I will take his persistent gripes with a pinch of salt. But anyway, I haven't bought Guzim any new clothes. I was referring to those hideously un-suitable tee-shirts and pullovers that Barry in-sists on gifting me every Christmas."

"Phew, I thought for a moment you were going soft in the head, dear," Marigold said with relief. "Don't worry; you get off to work, dear. I'll sort Guzim out with Barry's unwanted Yuletide offerings later. It will be nice for him to have something that is clean for a change when he is reunited with his wife. His ignorance of English will render him clueless as far as the joke captions are concerned."

"I do find Barry's idea of a Christmas joke a tad vulgar," I said.

About to take my departure, I was pulled up short when Marigold emitted a high-pitched screech. As I rushed to her side, fearing some in-jury had befallen her, Marigold shrieked, "The shower. It completely slipped my mind that Guzim only has an outdoor shower."

"That's one way of describing a leaky hose-pipe," I remarked.

I couldn't believe that Marigold had come

over all histrionic because it had belatedly dawned on her that Guzim's showering set-up was a tad primitive.

"You're missing the point, Victor. Guzim surely can't expect his wife to shower outside under a hosepipe. No woman should be expected to conduct her ablutions in such a crude manner."

"She may well be used to a similar arrangement back in Albania," I argued.

"Perhaps their Albanian hosepipe isn't overlooked," Marigold said, pursing her lips and pointing towards Kyria Maria's house.

"Ah, I get your drift. Papas Andreas may get more than he bargained for when he throws his shutters open. Even if Guzim's wife does look like the back end of a bus, it would still be cruel to put the temptation of a near naked woman hose piping herself off under the nose of a celibate cleric," I said.

"I was thinking more along the lines of the poor woman not wanting an audience…Victor, do you remember if we brought any old shower curtains over to Greece with us?" Marigold asked.

"Why on earth would we have dragged shower curtains to Greece? It would make no sense as you had already selected our new bathroom fittings, including a shower cubicle, before we packed for the off."

"Well, I may have thrown a couple in just on the off-chance…"

"The off-chance of what? The mind boggles," I sighed.

Ignoring me, Marigold instructed her sidekick, "Doreen, have a good rummage through these bin bags and see if you can turn up a shower curtain."

"I do enjoy a good rummage," Doreen declared, throwing herself into the task with gusto. Clearly the woman didn't associate the bag she was rifling through as being one of those I had rescued from the bins the previous evening; otherwise she wouldn't have gone near it without the rubber protection of a pair of Marigolds.

"Found one," Doreen announced triumphantly, holding aloft a drab shower curtain featuring images of avocados. I cringed at the sight, recalling that back in the 1970s Marigold had insisted it was the height of fashion to match the fruity plastic curtain with our then avocado bathroom suite. I was inordinately relieved that home décor trends had moved on since then.

"I'm off," I announced. "It wouldn't do for

me to be tardy on my first day. Don't forget to defrost the rabbit *stifado* for later."

"And don't forget to pretend that it's chicken in case Ashley has an aversion to eating bunnies," Marigold said.

"Rightio, chicken it is." Anything for a quiet life.

"Have a nice day at work, dear, and do try not to be late home. Geraldine is due to arrive this afternoon if they don't hit too much traffic from Athens."

The reminder of Geraldine's imminent arrival was almost enough to take the spring out of my step as I made my way to the shop. All thoughts of our annoying houseguest fled from my mind as the garbage truck came hurtling round the corner, forcing me to press myself into the hedgerow to avoid being mown down by the stinky wagon. The two chaps balancing on the rear plate next to the loading hopper made apologetic gestures. Plucking a couple of sharp burrs from the seat of my trousers, I waved in greeting, thinking I wouldn't do their job for all the tea in China.

Crossing the village square, I noticed that the padlocked bicycles that I had spotted yesterday were still there. The next moment, the incongruous sight of an orange nylon tent pitched under a plane tree, caught my eye. Such an eyesore really wasn't on: there must be some kind of local ordinance prohibiting campers from setting up tents wherever the fancy took them. Spotting one of the youngish men that had been in the taverna the previous evening filling a water bottle from the village tap, I put two and two together, deducing the tent and the bicycles must belong to the men who had been after local accommodation.

"You can't just pitch up here, it isn't a campsite, you know," I called over, tutting loudly to express my disapproval. It really wasn't on; if this sort of thing was allowed then in no time at all it would be a free for all, with motley collections of tents, bivouacs, camper vans and caravans despoiling the natural beauty of the peaceful setting, campers de-manding that the local *Dimarcheio* splash out on unsightly Porta Potties.

"Sorry about that, we did plan to move on and look for a room but Sean got a puncture. Difficult to fix in the dark. We'll be on our way as soon as we've had a coffee. Does that place we were in last night do breakfast?"

"No, Nikos will be hard at work in his fields

by now. You can get coffee at the village shop, but tidy that tent away first. You don't want to get lynched by a bunch of Greek pensioners mistaking you for a couple of gypsies," I said, reassured that the tent was just temporary.

"Rightio, we'll pack the tent away and then head to the shop for coffee. Thanks mate."

Pleased that the camper had heeded my words without demanding written proof of an ordinance banning random camping, I continued on my way. Even though I had yet to commence my training, I was already bringing customers to the shop. I hoped that Tina would appreciate what an asset I was.

Chapter 8

A Tad Judgemental

Tina, bundled up in a thick sweater beneath her pinny, was sweeping the pavement outside the shop. I assumed from her attire that she shared Nikos' opinion that September was winter. Tina's face lit up with a smile as I greeted her, clearly relieved that I hadn't let her down by bottling out of working in the shop at the last minute and that my punctuality was not governed by Greek time.

Pointing towards the tent with her broom,

Tina voiced her disapproval. "I must to telephone the *Dimarcheio* to remove the vagrants."

I suppressed a snort at Tina's overly stressed pronunciation, amused that she rhymed the first syllable of vagrants with rag. I didn't bother to correct her; we would never get any vital shop work done if I spent the day schooling her in correct English usage. My own pronunciation of Greek was still very much a work in progress rather than honed to perfection: ironically, considering my new occupation, *psonia*, the Greek word for shopping, was one of the words whose pronunciation remained a tongue twisting challenge.

"They're actually a couple of Scottish cyclists who pitched up their tent due to a puncture. They're taking their tent down now and then heading here for coffee. I recommended it."

"You will be good for the business, Victor. Not even the eight o'clock and you bring to me the new customer," Tina trilled with delight. "I must to show you how to make the coffee for them, yes."

"Yes, I think you'll need to," I concurred, assuming that making coffee Greek style most likely wouldn't involve much kettle boiling.

Leading me into a small cluttered kitchen at

the back of the shop, Tina grabbed a large packet of *Bravo* and demonstrated the fine art of brewing *Ellinko kafe* in a *briki* balanced on an ancient gas burner, running through the varying measures of sugar that I would need to add to the various orders.

"Let me see if I have this right," I said. "*Sketo* is no sugar, *metrio* is one sugar, and *glykos* is two."

"Not to forget the *variglykos*," Tina added.

"What's that?"

"The very sweet."

"So, how many sugars do I add to one of those?"

"The lot."

Tina's rather non-specific answer left me wishing that Greek customers could simply be served with a cup of coffee and left to spoon their own sugar in from a handy sugar bowl. Alas, that was not the traditional way.

"If they want the milk in the *kafe*, they to order *me gala*. Use the evaporate tin," Tina added. "Most to drink with not the milk."

"*Horis gala*," I said, smugly demonstrating I was up on the terminology, no great wonder considering I take my own coffee without sugar and milk. Recalling Vangelis adding cold water to Nescafe powder and giving it a vigorous shake, I added, "And the *frappé*. I'm guessing that is a doddle?"

"The doddle, I not to understand."

"*Efkolos*," I said, offering the Greek word for easy as a translation of doddle.

"It is the *Septemvrios*. No the one want the ice coffee in the winter," Tina said dismissively.

"But surely I should know how to make it just in case someone wants it," I argued, knowing the temperature was forecast to hit the 30s no matter how many bulky layers Tina insisted on wearing.

"It can to get the complicate if they want the *frappé* with the evaporate. It is the more the doddle to tell them you have the run out of the Nescafe," Tina advised, testing out her new English word and blithely overlooking the simple fact that she had many jars of the popular brand of instant cluttering up the shelves. Considering I had enough on my plate remembering how to fix *metrio* and *variglyko* to Tina's exacting standards, I reasoned that a customer going without their *frappé* wasn't the end of the world.

"And pour the glass of the water to go with the *kafe* from the bottle you to fill from the village tap; the spring water is the better than the nasty water from the sink."

Looking at the half-empty five litre storage container, I realised I might have to schlep out to the tap in the square on a regular basis, leaving the shop unattended. Just the thought of the complicated intricacies involved in serving Greek coffee correctly left me exhausted.

The ding of the shop bell indicated the arrival of customers. Tina appeared in no great rush to attend to them, preferring to point out the filthy looking rag earmarked for wiping down the outside tables and the *tavli* boards. I made a mental note to bin the germ laden sponges and cloths and help myself to new stock the moment Tina's back was turned. By the time we returned to the shop, the place was empty. I assumed that an impatient customer had got tired of waiting but Tina pointed out that they may be seated outside, expecting to be served coffee. It seemed that I would need to acquire the knack of being in two places at once.

Peering outdoors, I spotted Kyrios Stavropoulos, a local pensioner, claiming a table. Clad in a thick wool jacket, I surmised he hadn't bothered to keep abreast of the latest weather forecast. The dog-eared newspaper he was clutching would be of no use if he wanted an up to date forecast since it was more than a week out of date. From casual observation, I had noticed the elderly gentleman, along with his ancient cronies, sitting outside the shop for hours at a time nursing coffee or *ouzo* whilst arguing over a game of backgammon. Giving the evil eye to strangers was clearly an art they had honed to perfection, but I knew that a simple smile and *kalimera* would melt their frosty countenances in an instant.

"Excellent. I think we have our first coffee customer," I said to Tina. "I can put my new coffee making skills into practice."

"No need to ask the order, he drink the *glykos* every the day," Tina informed me before filling me in that the coffee drinkers must wait to be served if there was a queue of customers in the shop: paying customers took precedence over anyone with enough time on their hands to sit around. Her strategy explained why I was often kept waiting a good half-hour for a cup of coffee outside.

Kyrios Stavropoulos' coffee almost ended up all down Giannis the bee man's tee-shirt as the pair of us clashed in the shop doorway, Giannis weighed down with a large cardboard box. Leaving Tina to attend to the honeyed local,

I greeted the two Scottish campers by asking them how many sugars they fancied in their coffee. Disappointed when I disclosed that the shop didn't serve breakfast, they beamed with relief when I suggested they add a packet of 7Days ready-made chocolate stuffed croissants to their order.

"The Giannis was to bringing his the honey for me to sell. You must to telephone him if the stock to run low," Tina advised as Giannis departed.

"He looked a bit glum," I pointed out.

"Glum, I not to understand," Tina replied.

"Not very happy. He's usually very cheerful," I clarified.

"The Poppy go back to the university in the Scotland. The Giannis to miss her."

"Ah, young love," I said, wondering how long it would be before Giannis replaced Poppy on his pillion with some other beauty. There again, he could prove faithful. They certainly made a handsome couple: Giannis with his unruly dark locks and deep brown eyes, Poppy so striking she had been mistaken for a supermodel.

The two young Scots, shuffling rather uncomfortably under the unwavering glower of

V.D. BUCKET

Kyrios Stavropoulos, looked rather askance to be served miniscule cups of strong Greek coffee rather than mugs of instant. I pointed out that we were rather off the beaten track where current fads such as fashionable coffee and all day breakfasts had not yet encroached on traditional ways. They dutifully laughed when I quipped that the Greek idea of a hearty breakfast was a black coffee and a cigarette, their laughter drawing a frown of disapproval from Kyrios Stavropoulos. The pensioner clearly expected peace and quiet to reign as he perused his dated and dog-eared copy of *Rizospastis*, the daily newspaper put out by the Communist Party. Between the scowling pensioner and the inadequate coffee I served, it seemed that the village square was looking less idyllic as an impromptu campsite by the minute.

When a truck arrived with a beer delivery, Tina disappeared out the back to attend to it, leaving me in charge of the shop. Relieved that I wasn't expected to haul heavy crates, I was instead left to curse over the temperamental vagaries of the till which Tina had not yet taught me to use. Dealing with the first few early morning stragglers, I soon mastered the art of giving the cash drawer a good thump to get it to open.

BUCKET TO GREECE (VOL. 8)

To my utter consternation the till was devoid of any small change, not a solitary one or two cent coins in evidence. I became quite flustered when Panos' purchases came to 98 cents and I had no change to give him. About to ask Panos to wait whilst I went and asked Tina to cough up some change, he gruffly pointed out that the shop never gave change, ever: surely I had noticed. It dawned on me that I had been on the receiving end of Tina having no change on countless occasions, a situation she got round by conveniently rounding my bill up to the nearest 10 cents. It had never previously occurred to me that Tina kept the till devoid of small coins as a deliberate ploy to up her takings. Nevertheless, I found myself flushing with embarrassment when depriving the customers of their legitimate one or two cents worth of change. At least the coffees sold for a round one Euro, sparing me the embarrassment of being unable to offer change. There again, I reflected, if we sold the coffee for 99 cents, the customers may be more inclined to leave the balance from a one Euro coin as a tip.

Barry and Vangelis wandered in to place an order for a couple of takeaway *frappés*, the pair of them looking at me as though I had lost my marbles when I advised them we didn't serve iced beverages in winter.

"It is not the winter, Victor, it is only *Septemvrios*," Vangelis announced, despite the fact that he was already wrapped up in a thick fleece shirt.

"Victor is just trying to worm his way out of it because he doesn't know how to make it. He never touches instant," Barry laughed.

"*Tina, prepei na mathete ton Victor na kanei frappé,*" Vangelis shouted the moment Tina entered the shop, demanding that she teach me how to make his favourite coffee. It appeared that to Vangelis, going without his *frappé* was indeed the end of the world. The four of us squashed into the too-small kitchen where Tina reluctantly demonstrated the fine art of *frappé* making, telling Vangelis that he must make it himself if I was rushed off my feet once she was stuck at the hospital with Despina.

"But make sure you scrub your hands first, I don't want you leaving builder's grime all over the kitchen," I warned Vangelis, whilst Barry stepped back in the shop to answer his mobile phone.

"I think Marigold has lost the plot," Barry complained the second he hung up. "She's demanding I drop everything and head over to yours to nail up a shower curtain. You have a perfectly decent shower cubicle, what's she thinking of?"

"I expect she wants you to fix it up outdoors so that Guzim's wife will have privacy when she showers under the hosepipe," I explained. "She's a tad worried that Papas Andreas may get more than he bargained for when he throws open his shutters."

"I haven't got time for this, we have a busy workload today sorting the floor in your *apothiki*," Barry sighed. Despite his protestations, I knew he would be heading straight over to do Marigold's bidding as soon as he had a spare moment in his schedule; he could never say no to his sister. "There are times when I wish that she'd married someone who didn't bodge every attempt at DIY."

"There's no need to get personal, Barry," I retorted, cut to the quick. "I'll have you know that I successfully fixed a new shelf to the wall in my home office only last week."

"And it hasn't fallen down yet?"

"There's no need to roll your eyes so dramatically. The shelf is still on the wall," I said, crossing my fingers behind my back. I hadn't actually gone as far as testing the shelf out yet by placing anything on it. I wanted to give it a good few days for the industrial strength super glue to set.

"Speak of the devil," Barry hissed, nudging me sharply and showering the front of my shirt with iced coffee as Papas Andreas entered the shop.

"I don't think that's a polite way of referring to a cleric," I snapped, dabbing at the coffee smudge with a filthy floor cloth. "Must you be so clumsy, Barry? I'll have to borrow one of Tina's aprons now to cover the stain."

"I didn't have the Papas down as a morning tippler," Barry hissed, watching Andreas select a bottle of cheap plastic red from the shelf.

"I wonder if I ought to warn him that Geraldine will be turning up later today," I mused.

"I wouldn't risk it. He might get weepy," Barry warned.

"Perhaps I'll keep schtum; they might not even run into one another. Speaking of Geraldine, I don't suppose I can persuade you and Cynthia to join us for dinner this evening, dilute the numbers so to speak."

"No chance, there's no point inviting marital strife by putting Cynthia and Geraldine in the same room. I told you, Cyn didn't take to her," Barry said, clamming up as Papas Andreas approached the till with his bottle. "*Ela* Vangeli, we'd best get a wiggle on if we're going to squeeze Marigold in."

Casting a wink in my direction, Vangelis did a quick on the spot jiggle to demonstrate his understanding of Barry's slang. I chortled as the pair of them shimmied out of the shop, leaving the Papas looking less than impressed with their ungainly moves. Combing his unruly beard with his fingers, Andreas looked a tad shifty as he paid for the wine and a packet of chewing gum.

"*To krasi einai yia ti mitera mou,*" Andreas said, telling me that the wine was for his mother. It was no business of mine why he was buying wine; it was after all a shop. However, his seeming desperation to disassociate himself from his purchase made me consider that perhaps there was a grain of truth to Barry's words about the Papas being a morning tippler. Perchance Marigold had already let the cat out of the bag about Geraldine's impending visit and the news had driven the Papas to drink. There again, recalling Kyria Maria's previous filthy habit of burning plastic every morning, perhaps it was my elderly neighbour who was rather partial to a bottle of cheap plonk. It struck me that she would need to be half-cut to endure the toxic smell.

Athena rushed in and grabbed a packet of *kourabiedes* and a tell-tale bag of icing sugar. It didn't take a genius to surmise that she intended to sprinkle the icing sugar on top of the shop bought almond cookies and pass them off as her own. Of course, I wasn't crass enough to comment when a raised eyebrow would do. I knew that Marigold would be delighted to be informed of this development since Athena swore blind the cookies she served to her hairdressing clientele were fresh from her oven.

Beginning to get into the swing of shop work, I realised I had taken to it like a duck to water. However, I hadn't anticipated the scolding that ensued from Tina once Athena departed. Apparently, it had not gone unnoticed that I had a rather judgemental way of raising my eyebrows and rolling my eyes at our customers' purchases.

"You must to be the discreet like the doctor, Victor. You must to make the pretend you not to see what they buy."

About to protest that she had me all wrong, I recalled that I had indeed amused myself by chuckling when the resident village vegetarian, the German hippie, Heinrich, bought a packet of pork sausages. It was also true that I had indeed raised my eyebrows at the sheer hypocrisy of the eco-conscious hippie purchasing liquid Ajax rather than using environmentally friendly vinegar and a lemon to clean his house. I had also found it difficult to control my mirth when Mathias, the garlic chomping brother of Litsa, bought a packet of mouth freshening mints, perchance seemingly aware that his garlic breath announced his presence at twenty paces.

Tina's tactful reprimand made me belatedly realise that it wouldn't be good for business if the customers, imagining that I was being hypercritical of the contents of their baskets, took their custom elsewhere. Taking Tina's criticism to heart, I determined to slap a look of complete indifference on my face no matter what the customers chose to sling in their baskets. I determined to be so blasé that my utter discretion would give a priest in the confessional a run for his money.

Chapter 9

The Germ of an Idea

The rest of the morning flew by. The two Scottish cyclists pleasantly surprised me by leaving a generous tip, something I knew from my experience of cheffing in the taverna that none of the locals were likely to do. Whilst the regular taverna goers had demonstrated a marked reluctance to part with even the smallest of coins as a token of their appreciation, they had more than made up for it by showering me with fruit and vegetables from their gardens, in addition to local offerings such as honey, newly laid eggs, illicitly brewed *tsipouro* and rough-hewn blocks of handmade olive oil soap.

Kyrios Stavropoulos' elderly Greek cronies joined him, claiming their regular seats outside. Once I had served them coffee, I left them to their own devices. Since each of them could make one tiny Greek coffee last an interminable amount of time, there was no need for pesky refills. After several hours of toiling, I grabbed a mid-morning coffee, taking a brief breather outside in the sunshine, more than aware that I didn't have the luxury of spinning my own beverage out over several hours. The day was sunny and clear, so hot that Kyrios Stavropoulos soon reluctantly shrugged off his thick woollen jacket to reveal a faded Che Guevara tee-shirt, quite fitting considering his out of date Communist reading material.

I reluctantly downed my coffee in one when my good friend Dimitris arrived, the gentle professor immediately attracting slanderous insults from Kyrios Stavropoulos. The latter accused Dimitris of being a traitor to *Kommounistiko Komma Elladas,* the Communist Party of Greece, along with other barbs that were beyond my comprehension but seemed to centre round Dimitris' habit of wearing his long hair tied back in a ponytail. Fearing I may be called upon to break up an unseemly fist fight between the two men, I grabbed Tina's broom, hoping I wouldn't be called upon to wield it as a weapon. Fortunately, Kyrios Stavropoulos was too riddled with arthritis to make good on the threats he was firing at my friend; he was nothing but hot air and bluster when it came to the crunch.

Dimitris rose above the fracas with quiet dignity, telling me he was tempted to visit Apostolos for a short back and sides since his long hair threw a question mark over his political leanings. Dimitris had been politically disengaged even before his unjust incarceration under the Junta, but retaining a hairstyle associated with a political party he eschewed left him wide open to verbal harassment. By the time Dimitris left the shop clutching a treat for his pig, the bevy of coffee drinking pensioners outside were too engrossed in a heated political argument amongst themselves to turn on the professor.

I enjoyed the opportunity to practice my Greek on the non-English speaking villagers that popped in the shop. Most of the regulars readily tolerated my ignorance when I couldn't direct them to the exact spot on the shelf where an elusive item was stocked. They appeared indulgent of my lack of proficiency with the cheese slicer, graciously accepting uneven lumps without too many complaints. Litsa made a great fuss of plastering my finger when the cheese slicer got the better of me, but she did refuse the blood splattered slice of *kefalotyri* before I had chance to wrap it. In my defence, I had failed to notice the crimson smear.

As noon approached, Norman wandered in, scowling at the shelves with a look of blank exasperation. Spotting me positioned behind the till, he went on the attack, saying in a querulous tone, "This is all your wife's fault."

"What has Marigold done now?" I asked, fearing the worst.

"She's dragged Doreen over to yours for the day. I've just had to cart her sewing machine over there. They've rigged it up outside that shed of yours in the garden."

"The shed is nothing to do with me, it belongs to Guzim," I protested.

"Well, it's most inconvenient for Doreen to disappear at this time of day. I will have to make my own lunch," Norman complained peevishly. Holding an aubergine aloft, he added, "Any idea what I do with one of these?"

"You could roast it in the oven with tomatoes and *feta*, and perhaps a pinch of herbs," I suggested.

"Sounds a bit complicated, can't say I know how to work the oven. Could I put it in a sandwich?"

"Well, not raw, you'd need to cook it first," I advised, watching Norman hold the vegetable with great caution as though it was about to explode. I was beginning to feel a tad peckish myself, but the thought of an aubergine sandwich rather killed my appetite. "Perhaps cheese and tomato would be a better choice for a sandwich. Those tomatoes are fresh in this morning, you won't find tastier ones."

"This one's a whopper, I'll take it," Norman decided, scrutinising a single tomato as though not quite sure what to do with it. "I can never quite get over the size of them over here, abnormally enormous and the oddest shapes. You think this one would be good in a sandwich?"

"I'm sure it's an excellent choice." Realising that recommending items for sale must be part and parcel of my duties, I wondered if I ought to steer him towards something more expensive to give the shop's takings a hefty boost. I decided to up-sell instead, suggesting Norman purchase a jar of *angourakia toursi* to liven up his sandwich.

"What's that, then?"

"Pickled cucumbers."

"Think I'll give them a miss, the vinegar might make the bread go soggy," Norman proclaimed after a lengthy deliberation. "Not my department, this cooking lark. I leave all that to Doreen."

Biting my lip, I swallowed the sardonic comment on the tip of my tongue: *Have you tasted your wife's cooking?*

Having been subjected to more than one of Doreen's dinner parties, I was all too aware how culinary challenged she was, tending to serve up slop that had pretensions far beyond her inept kitchen skills; just the memory of her botched Peking duck had me reaching for the indigestion remedy. Mindful of Tina's advice about not appearing judgemental of the customers, I took a tactful approach, asking Norman, "Don't you get bored with Doreen's cooking?"

"Well, we do eat out a couple of times a week. There are some good tavernas down on the coast. Doreen isn't keen on the local place because she likes to dress up for dinner and make it a bit of an occasion."

"We like Nikos' taverna, though it's true that one has to dress down rather than up when dining there," I said, thinking one of its advantages was that I knew for sure that I was unlikely to run into Norman there.

"Well, it's different for you. You speak a bit of Greek. Doreen and I feel a bit out of it, with not knowing the language," Norman moaned, as though getting to grips with Greek was completely out of his hands. "We like to socialise a bit when we're out. Down on the coast, we often run into English tourists we can have a chat with."

Or latch onto and bore silly with your endless obsession with traffic cones. Mindful once again of Tina's earlier admonishment, I didn't voice my thoughts, though it struck me that Norman was in danger of morphing into a soberer version of Harold if he started trawling the tourist areas looking for willing victims to bore. I would need to have a serious talk with him if he started to get ideas about installing a pool.

"I might as well take some *ouzo* to wash the tomato down," Norman said, grabbing a bottle. I was rather taken aback: I had never had Norman down as much of a drinker. Certainly he had always limited his alcohol consumption at the expat dinner parties. I wondered if the boredom of retirement was finally getting to him. "Right, that's everything I need for lunch. Our daughter popped a video in the post; at least I'll have something to watch this afternoon."

"A video of the family back in England?" I asked.

"No, I got her to record the latest series of 'The Bill'; it will give me something to do. I just hope Doreen's back before dinner; I don't fancy having to make myself tomato sandwiches twice in one day."

"Perhaps you should buy two tomatoes, just on the off-chance," I suggested.

For a brief moment, I felt a tad sorry for Norman, before realising how pathetic he actually was. Unlike his wife, Norman appeared to have nothing constructive to occupy his time. At least Doreen took great pride in cultivating her flower garden and threw herself into Greek dancing lessons with Marigold, not to mention the two women were always off having coffee with the neighbours or rushing off to the local sewing circle.

Norman had no one to blame but himself if he chose to eat his wife's dreadful cooking rather than experiment in the kitchen. After all, he had nothing but spare time on his hands since retiring. In contrast, my spare time was severely restricted due to my juggling part time employment with rearing a clutch of chickens and penning the Bucket saga.

During my illustrious career as a public health inspector back in Manchester, my long working hours had meant that the bulk of the cooking fell on my wife's shoulders. Whilst Marigold's cooking was certainly adequate, it definitely lacked imagination, something I had been happy to inject into our meals since moving to Greece by taking over the reins in the kitchen. There was no reason at all why Norman could not emulate my example. I found it immensely satisfying to use locally grown or reared produce in Greek recipes, becoming ever more adventurous in my gastronomic creations. By now, I was way beyond the stage of kitchen novice: though I hate to blow my own trumpet, I have become quite the competent chef.

A germ of an idea began to form in my mind. The job in the shop was only temporary, until Despina recovered from her op. With the rest of the winter to while away, I could perhaps run cookery courses in my kitchen, charging a premium price to pass on my knowledge of

Greek cooking to complete lemons like Norman. Of course, I would need to research potential demand but I rather thought I could be on to something.

My ruminations were interrupted by Sherry breezing in: I had been so wrapped up in my thoughts that I hadn't even noticed Norman's departure.

"Sherry, tell me, do you do much Greek cooking?" I asked.

"I'd jolly well like to but I'm always afraid I'll make a hash of it. Henry used to say I had a knack for burning water," she brayed, exposing her prominent teeth as she threw her head back in a horsey laugh.

"So what do you cook at home?"

"Well, to be honest, I don't really cook, though I am a dab hand with a tin opener and the toasted sandwich maker. I'm reluctant to admit it but I do rather rely on deliveries from the jolly old British Corner Shop."

"So if Greek cookery lessons were available…"

"That would be spiffing, I'd sign up for them in a jiffy," she trilled, plonking a sliced loaf and a packet of imported processed cheese slices on the counter. Clearly she was having an unimaginative toastie for lunch.

Both Norman and Sherry had certainly given me food for thought. Stocking the fridge with cartons of milk and tubs of Greek yoghurt, my mind wandered as I mulled over the viability of setting up cookery classes. The idea had legs. The downside was the type of expat student I would inevitably attract. I would have to decide if it was worth it to have the likes of Norman and Sherry littering my kitchen.

Chapter 10

Victor has an Eric Flynn Moment

V ictor, did you to move the packets of cakes?" Tina asked me, noticing the empty space on the counter.

"I didn't move them, I sold them," I said proudly, pleased that I had managed, with a bit of persuasion, to shift the perilously close to its sell-by date stock to the gullible Sherry and offload the rest of the cakes on Dimitris to feed to his pig.

"I can see you will be the good for business even though you have not to work in the shop before."

"I have some experience selling on market stalls," I modestly admitted, recalling my success in shifting Panos' *vlita*.

"I remember the Panos to tell me you draw the crowd with your speak," Tina said with a smile.

"We call it the gift of the gab in English," I said, keen for Tina to pick up a few idioms.

Seemingly delighted with my progress, Tina insisted I take a lunch break, reminding me that I would be unable to indulge in such luxuries once she was away at the hospital. Promising to return in an hour, I made a mental note to bring myself a packed lunch once I was left solely in charge.

Returning home for my short break, I was surprised to discover an electric cable stretched across the garden, leading to Doreen's sewing machine. Barely pausing to take her foot off the pedal, Marigold's sidekick told me that she was knocking up a frilly valance to go round the base of Guzim's bed. Although I wasn't convinced that psychedelic orange lent itself to frills, I kept my own counsel; after all, I wasn't the one that would have to sleep with it.

"You can't go wrong with a nice valance. I've

done a matching fabric cover to throw over the rabbit cage," Doreen said.

"Doruntina has a cage? I thought it slept with Guzim."

"You do have the strangest notions, Victor. Whoever heard of a grown man sleeping with a rabbit?" Doreen scoffed, a dismissive blink of her eyes accompanying her words. Considering we were in my garden, I determined to have the last word.

"Keep up the good word," I huffed. Hoping that my wife was around to prepare me a spot of lunch, I asked, "Have you seen Marigold?"

"She's in the shed. She's giving it a lick of paint," Doreen replied, narrowing her eyes to thread the needle on the machine.

Cautiously edging my way past Guzim's iron bedstead and his dented old fridge, both tatty items littering my garden, I made my way to the shed. Our old aubergine embellished shower curtain was now tacked to one side of the shed, concealing Guzim's leaky hosepipe. Whilst I considered the arrangement a tad unsightly, I realised it had its advantages. In addition to sparing Andreas the sight of Guzim's wife showering, it would spare any of our future houseguests suffering the rude awakening of Guzim hosing himself down in his under-pants.

Contrary to what Doreen had said, Mari-gold wasn't actually giving the shed a lick of paint. Rather, she was directing her brother who was stuck up a ladder, paintbrush in hand, on the receiving end of Marigold's barked orders.

"I didn't expect to find you here, Barry. I thought you had a full workload on," I ex-claimed in surprise, irritated that he wasn't hard at work in the *apothiki*. Surveying the paintwork, I wondered how Guzim would react when he came home to discover the walls of his hovel now a sickly bubblegum pink.

"Have you tried saying no to my sister?" Barry snapped, having clearly been roped in to help against his will.

"What are you doing here, dear? Have you to come to help?" Marigold asked.

"Don't try and rope me in too. I just popped home for lunch. I haven't got long; I don't sup-pose you have prepared any food."

"Really, Victor, you can see that I'm up to my eyes in it. Surely you're not so helpless that you can't fix yourself a spot of lunch," Marigold retorted. About to protest that although I was in no way helpless, it really wasn't expecting too much for my wife to knock up some lunch whilst I was out earning a crust, I stopped short. Inwardly berating myself, I thought, *you sound as pathetic as Norman. You don't need your wife to cook your lunch; you are a strong independent man who has mastered all the kitchen appliances.*

"What made you choose pink?" I belatedly asked, thinking it really wasn't a colour that I could see appealing to Guzim. "I seem to recall Guzim objecting to a cast-off pink shirt because he considered the particular shade unmanly."

"I had a job lot going spare from Sherry's place..." Barry said.

"It doesn't matter what Guzim thinks, we are doing this to give his poor downtrodden wife a semblance of comfort," Marigold interrupted.

"Well, I wouldn't expect him to be grateful, if I were you. Turning a man's home into a frilly pink palace may be taking things a tad too far."

"Nonsense, pink is a very soothing colour," Marigold argued.

"Not when you pair it with psychedelic orange," I retorted. Deciding to leave them to it, I turned on my heel, almost electrocuting Doreen as I tripped over the sewing machine lead. Doreen's cry of outrage brought Marigold running. Whilst Doreen rushed to put the plug back in the extension cable, I took the opportunity to discreetly ask Marigold if she'd noticed that Norman was turning into a day drinker.

"Whatever keeps him out of Doreen's hair," Marigold hissed. "If Norman had his way, they'd be one of those dreadful couples living in each other's pockets twenty-four hours a day. It's such a relief that you have your little hobbies to keep you from getting under my feet."

Shaking my head in bewilderment at Marigold's blinkered view that my slaving away in the shop could be considered a little hobby, I flounced off towards the house. My irritation waned when Marigold called out that Panos had dropped off a humongous watermelon for me. The refreshing fruit was just the ticket for a tasty *feta* and *karpouzi* salad, garnished with juicy black Kalamata olives and fresh mint leaves.

The promised watermelon had been left on the doorstep. I presumed that Marigold had been unable to lift it and had been reluctant to invite Panos to carry it indoors, not wanting his mucky wellies traipsing all over her newly mopped floor. Hoisting the heavy melon onto my shoulder, I carried it into the kitchen, the sheer size of the fruit presenting the conundrum of how open it. Dithering between attacking the watermelon with a large serrated knife or a meat cleaver, I rather dramatically imagined slashing it open with a sword. Rather fancying myself as a dashing Errol Flynn swashbuckler type doing a bit of nifty swordwork, I brought the meat cleaver down on the melon with a hearty slash, crying, "Take that." My swashbuckling fantasy ended in a damp squib when the kitchen hatchet became firmly lodged in the melon.

The only way I could dislodge the cleaver was by putting the watermelon on the floor, placing my foot on one side of the fruit and heaving: a clumsy landing on my posterior put an end to my Errol Flynn flights of fancy. With the cleaver finally free, I used physical force to prise the melon in two, the ruby juices leaking all over Marigold's newly mopped floor. Fortunately the cats came to my rescue, licking up every lost drop as I set to creating my salad, dressing it with a tangy mix of freshly squeezed lemon and extra virgin olive oil. For once, Marigold's precious imported domestics had earned their keep; I duly rewarded them both by filling their bowls with chunks of the refreshing fruit.

Tucking into the delicious salad, I reflected

that I was certainly no Errol Flynn. The nearest thing to a swashbuckling sword fight in these remote parts of the Mani had been when one of Guzim's Albanian cronies had put another compatriot in the hospital by slashing him with his *Rugovo* dance sword. As I recalled the unfortunate incident, I remembered Spiros' warning that Besnik may be involved with some shady characters: there had certainly been something dodgy about the sword wielding labourer that Besnik had employed. Hoping that there was nothing concrete to Spiros' fears, I realised that I had perchance been a bit too quick to dismiss them. Besnik was due to drive Guzim's wife to Meli and I didn't relish the prospect of him bringing any trouble to the Bucket household.

Sated with watermelon and cheese, I returned to the shop for my afternoon shift with renewed vigour. The elderly Greek men outside the shop, having finally polished off their coffees, were now nursing cloudy glasses of ouzo prior to staggering home for the afternoon siesta. Although Tina occasionally closed the shop during siesta hours, she told me that she preferred to remain open on the off-chance of catching any passing trade. At this time of year the area attracted foreign walkers and cyclists tempted to explore off the beaten track.

"With your, how do you call it, the gift of the gab, you must to try and sell them the traditional Greek souvenir if they stop in for the bottle of water," Tina suggested.

"I didn't know that you sold souvenirs," I said in surprise, having failed to notice any popular tourist paraphernalia lining the shelves.

"The local *meli*, the Kalamata olives, the olive oil soap, the *ouzo* and *tsipouro*; these are the souvenir of the Greece, yes?"

"Indeed they are: I was thinking more along the lines of worry beads and mati jewellery," I said.

"You think I must to sell such things?"

"Well, tourists do like that kind of thing but it depends on how much tourist trade you get," I advised cautiously.

"You must to ask them if they would buy them…"

"You want me to ask any tourists that chance to wander in if they would buy things that we don't actually sell?"

"Yes, that would be the good. If there is the demand, I could to get some. I must to look at the way to bring in the more money." Lowering her voice to a whisper, Tina confided, "The *fake-laki* for the *Mama* knee was many the hundred *evro*."

"A terrible business," I said, sympathising with her position.

"*Ti na kanoume*?" A resigned shrug accompanied the invariable Greek fall back phrase of 'what can we do?'

Unscrupulous doctors demanding bribes in the form of small envelopes stuffed with cash, *fakelaki*, was an illegal yet common practice. I gathered it was pretty routine for local families to club together to pay the extorted price in order to facilitate a speedy operation for a relative. When I had voiced my disgust to Spiros about medical professionals holding ordinary Greeks to ransom in this way, my friend had assured me that I would be immune from the practice, telling me, "The doctor not to risk it with the foreign. The foreign may to report them. The Greek just to pay." I still considered such a practice disgraceful.

Tina asked if I felt comfortable holding the fort as she needed to pack for the trip to Athens since she would be busy in the shop the next day. After assuring her that she could leave me to it, she left me to my own devices. Since the shop was free of customers, I decided to make a start on a spot of scrubbing. Though hesitant to voice my criticisms to Tina, the place was looking decidedly grubby.

Searching for cleaning supplies in the stock room, I chanced upon a large cardboard box stuffed with wooden honey jars and dippers, identical to the one I had discovered amongst the pile of junk in the *apothiki*. I felt a tad foolish when I realised that I jumped to the conclusion that my precious find had been authentic and valuable when the label on the cardboard box revealed that the stock had been 'Made in China.'

Helping myself to a pair of Marigolds from the stock, I was soon hard at work emptying the shelves of bottles of spirits and wine in order to treat the shelves to a thorough sanitising. Meticulously wiping each bottle down with a wet cloth, I rearranged the stock to make the display more inviting by lining the bottles up in a colour coordinated pattern. My solitary task remained uninterrupted since amazingly the shop wasn't overrun with hordes of tourists demanding souvenirs.

Chapter 11

A Good Grasp of English

Tina, seemingly satisfied that I had grasped the basics of managing the shop, insisted that I call it a day once her niece, Thalia, arrived late afternoon. The teenager, slumped under the weight of an enormous backpack, came directly from her afternoon lesson at the *frontistirio* where she was studying English language in preparation for the advanced Cambridge examination. My suggestion to Thalia that I would be able to give her a few pointers if she became confused on the finer points of English grammar was met with a surly scowl: the teenager claimed she'd had quite enough of studying after enduring extra maths, physics, and English once the school released its pupils for the day. It struck me that the system was quite contrary: when the school finished around 2pm the children then rushed off to additional private lessons, their parents footing the bills.

Strolling home across the village square, the weight of the spare set of shop keys Tina had entrusted to me, jangled in my pocket, ready for opening on Thursday morning. Tina and her mother were leaving for Athens the next evening in order to be at the hospital bright and early on Thursday. Although Tina remained a tad apprehensive about leaving the shop, I assured her it was in capable hands. It wouldn't do for her to worry: she would have enough on her plate sleeping in a chair by Despina's hospital bed and running round after her unspeakable mother. Just because the bribe of a *fakelaki* was in play, it didn't excuse the patient's relatives from doing all of the donkey work.

After a solid nine hours of serving and schmoozing customers, scrubbing and stocking shelves, and botching coffee orders, I had a new respect for shop workers. Looking forward to putting my feet up, my mood soured when I recalled that the house would likely not be the haven of peace I was seeking as we were expecting Marigold's houseguests. Noticing the absence of a rental car outside, I sighed in relief, presuming they were caught up in traffic.

"Darling, I'm home," I called out to Marigold. "I gather Geraldine and her new fellow haven't turned up yet. I have to say it's a blessing because I'm in no mood for small talk after dealing with customers all day…"

Rather taken aback to discover a strange young woman sitting in the kitchen drinking tea with my wife, I abruptly clammed up, not wishing to put my foot in it. When I say a strange woman, I should of course clarify that I mean strange as in unknown rather than strange as in peculiar: any peculiarities would only be an assumption until introductions were made.

"Sorry, darling. I didn't realise you had company," I said, casting my eyes over the young woman. Marigold's visitor was perched rather nervously on the edge of her seat, her back ramrod straight. She appeared to be barely out of her teens with shoulder length brown hair neatly tied back to reveal an almost painfully thin pale face devoid of makeup, a smattering of freckles adding a touch of colour to her forehead and nose. The rather hesitant smile she gave me transformed her face from plain to almost pretty.

"Victor, this is Luljeta, Guzim's wife," Marigold said.

"How you do love to tease me, darling. You can't seriously expect me to believe that the toothless shed dweller managed to marry a girl who looks half-way normal," I blurted, thinking that Marigold was amusing herself by pulling my leg. "No one in their right mind would saddle themselves with Guzim unless they were pug ugly..."

Firing a withering look in my direction, Marigold interrupted, "Luljeta speaks English." As her words sank in, I abruptly curtailed my laughter, mortified beyond belief.

Ignoring my rude and tactless outburst with quiet grace, Luljeta extended a work worn hand, nails bitten down to the quick.

"It is a pleasure to meet you, Mr Bucket. Guzim tells me that you are very kind to him," Luljeta said. I couldn't help but stare, fascinated to discover that Guzim's wife wasn't nearly as toothless as I'd imagined, only missing the odd incisor.

I was gobsmacked to hear Guzim's wife speak slow and precise English, devoid of the typical surplus articles such as an excessive use of 'the' that the Greeks tended to pepper their English with. Clearly shy, Luljeta spoke with a quiet confidence.

"Well, I try to put a bit of gardening work Guzim's way and he does an excellent job with the chickens…" I blustered, desperately trying to cover my embarrassment and squirming uncomfortably under Luljeta's measured gaze.

"Luljeta has had a long and tiring journey, Victor," Marigold interrupted. Turning to Luljeta, she said, "Perhaps you would like to use our bathroom to freshen up, dear."

"That is very kind of you, Mrs Bucket," Luljeta said.

As soon as Marigold had shown Luljeta to the bathroom, I said, "I rather expected to come home to Doreen and instead I find Guzim's wife in our kitchen. Why is she in here instead of in the shed with her husband?"

"Doreen won't be here until seven, they got tied up at the museum, and Guzim hasn't come home yet. It felt a bit impolite to just direct her to his empty shed. Luljeta seems a bit out of her depth, after all, she is very young and it's the first time that she has ever left her village…and of course, Guzim hasn't seen the makeover yet."

"She can't be that young, she has five children," I countered before recalling that Guzim had confided that Luljeta had been a teenage bride. I supposed that even with five sprogs, she may still only be in her early twenties.

"The shed isn't the only thing that could do with a bit of a makeover," Marigold hissed. "Perhaps I should take Luljeta in hand and give her a few tips on style and makeup."

"I really don't think you should interfere, dear," I cautioned. "You may well embarrass the poor girl…their budget clearly doesn't run to fripperies."

"I suppose you're right but I can't help thinking that one of my old dresses and a bit of lippy could work wonders," Marigold sighed, just as Luljeta returned, awkwardly retaking her seat. I could see what my wife was getting at: Luljeta's plain cotton dress was shabby and drab with visible evidence of mending, hardly the sort of fashionable thing that the youngsters were wearing. Luljeta's dress hung from her thin frame, drowning her in its folds: despite Guzim's constant claims that his wife ate all his money, she didn't appear to waste it on excessive amounts of food.

"How long will you be staying?" I asked Luljeta.

"I don't know. I must wait until Besnik returns for me. I hate to leave the children…"

"Of course you do," Marigold interrupted. "And you have a new baby to think of."

Mention of the baby turned Luljeta weepy. Clearly self-conscious about breaking down in tears in front of two strangers, she struggled to contain her sobs. Grabbing the box of tissues which Marigold passed her, Luljeta blew her nose noisily, stuttering through strangled gasps, "I never wanted to leave my babies."

"It's an awfully long trip to make for a flying visit," I pointed out.

"I did not want to come. Besnik told me I must come with him to look after the rabbits. He became angry when I told him no. Besnik reminded me that he had done favours for our family and said that I owed him."

It struck me as a bit heavy handed of Besnik to exert pressure on this poor young mother who was clearly distraught to be separated from her children. I recalled that Besnik had some familial connection to Luljeta and that he had taken it upon himself to sort out Guzim's Greek paperwork and ease the flow of Guzim's wages to his wife in Albania. It appeared, from Luljeta's words, that Besnik had only extended a helping hand as a quid pro quo. Despite feeling perturbed by this, I did recall the random fact that the Latin phrase 'quid pro quo' translated to the same words in Greek: another bit of handy Greek vocabulary for my ever growing list.

"The trip from Albania took many hours. Once we crossed the border, Besnik refused to stop to let me tend to the rabbits. He told me that if we were stopped by the police, I must say that I was his wife. I was very frightened; I have no legal papers to be in Greece. Later, Besnik met some men and exchanged the truck with the rabbits for a car. He told me not to worry; the car had Greek plates."

Marigold and I exchanged worried looks at the thought that Besnik had taken advantage of this naïve girl, involving her in what sounded like some shady deal. Rabbits, my hat.

"Does Guzim know that you felt pressured by Besnik?" I asked solicitously.

"No, I have not spoken with my husband. We have no telephone at home; we rely on Besnik to pass messages."

"Well, Guzim is very excited that you are visiting him," Marigold assured the now blushing Luljeta.

"He is? I will be very happy to see my husband, I miss him very much."

"Guzim never mentioned that you have such a good grasp of English," I said, thinking that Guzim had said very little about Luljeta beyond his constant carping that she ate all his money.

"I spend many hours learning English. I have the radio and listen to the BBC world service. I want to teach English to the children. I think it will help my girls. I never had any opportunities; my family expected me to marry as soon as they found me a husband, but I want more for my daughters." A look of steely determination accompanied Luljeta's words.

"Guzim told me that you were a teenage bride," I said, curious to learn more details.

"It is the custom in my village. At first it was very difficult for me, I was very sad because my husband must work in a foreign country. Things are not easy in Albania and it was hard for me, a woman alone," Luljeta sighed. "Now that I am more mature, I can see that Guzim had no choice. He could not earn enough money to support his family unless he worked abroad. Now I put any money I can spare into the rabbits. Maybe one day, Fatos will run the farm without the need to work abroad, perhaps even build a house on the land."

With the unspoken assumption that her son would inherit the farm and Guzim's ready dismissal of girls as nothing more than inconvenient mouths to feed, I could see why Luljeta was resolved to give her daughters more opportunities. If she could successfully school them in languages it may well offer them other options than following in her footsteps of an arranged marriage and a subsistence life on a dirt farm.

"Well, I have to say that your English is excellent, Luljeta," Marigold cooed, clearly as surprised as I was that this ambitious young woman was married to Guzim. I made a mental note to give Guzim a pay rise.

The distinctive sound of Guzim's clapped out moped drifted upstairs.

"Guzim's back," I announced.

Thanking us for our hospitality, Luljeta ran her fingers over her hair to make sure it was tidy before rushing down to greet her husband, Marigold making a move to follow. Putting a steadying hand on my wife's arm, I counselled her, "Don't go interrupting their reunion. It's months since they've seen one another."

"I suppose you're right," Marigold sighed in annoyance, hurrying to the balcony to spy on the couple. "I'll give them five minutes but then I must show Guzim what I've done with his shed. The transformation is quite remarkable."

Chapter 12

The Great Shed Reveal

Marigold, beyond excited to show off the shed makeover, insisted that I accompany her to the bottom of the garden. I must say that I found Marigold's eagerness to intrude on the possibly romantic reunion of the Albanian shed dweller and his young wife quite uncharacteristically insensitive, particularly when she announced that she was going to telephone Doreen and tell her to rush over to get in on the action.

"I couldn't have done it without Doreen's

help, she's been quite marvellous. Such a whizz with the sewing machine," Marigold gushed as she waited for Doreen to answer the phone.

"That's nice, dear." I inwardly cringed, hoping that Marigold wouldn't insist on inviting her sidekick in for drinks after viewing the shed. It really was too much to expect me to make asinine small talk after a hard day slogging like a Trojan in the village store. "And are you intending to drag Barry over too and turn it into a party? After all, he slopped the paint on."

"Really, Victor, such sarcasm is most unbecoming. Barry has been slaving away in the *apothiki* most of the day and deserves to go home and put his feet up in peace."

Rolling my eyes at Marigold's tone-deaf statement, I wondered what she imagined I had been doing at the shop all day. "I've not exactly been lounging around with..."

"Shush, can't you see that I'm on the telephone," Marigold barked.

Even though I tuned out from her mindless phone chatter with Doreen, there was no blocking out the endless litanies of "Oh no," and "You don't say," punctuating their dialogue.

"Such a shame, Doreen can't make it. Apparently their kitchen resembles a gory murder scene; she says it's like something out of a slasher film…"

I tuned out again, my mind instantly filled with images of an *ouzo* sozzled Norman slashing his wife with a *Rugovo* dance sword. Although the image was quite satisfying, I realised it was ridiculously inapt. If Norman was inclined to do his wife in, he would no doubt choose a far more pedestrian murder weapon, most likely clubbing Doreen over the head with one of his precious traffic cones.

"Victor, are you even listening to me?" Marigold's words brought me out of my pleasant reverie. "I know that Doreen tends to exaggerate but you really would think that a grown man would know that tomatoes and a microwave oven aren't necessarily a good mix. Anyway, she's up to her elbows in Marigolds and Vim."

I made a mental note to keep Norman well away from tomatoes if I went ahead with my cookery classes. Still at least Norman's kitchen disaster spared Guzim from the indignity of an additional expat gawping at his humble abode. I imagine a collection of foreigners judging his hovel may make him feel like a zoo animal on display.

"Doreen has offered to help with the soft

furnishings for the *apothiki*. She has the most marvellous touch when it comes to turning our old curtains from Manchester into creatively unique cushions," Marigold said as we trooped outside.

"So you think make do and mend is good enough for my mother?" I bristled.

"It's not as though Violet Burke is renowned for having good taste," Marigold said defensively, reminding me about my mother's penchant for plastic fruit. "And it will spare your credit card. I do know how you hate to prise it loose from your wallet."

Catching sight of Guzim and Luljeta outside the shed, I made a point of slowing down to admire Marigold's herb garden. Rubbing a stem of thyme between my fingers, I inhaled the aromatic scent, the smell reminding me that we would soon be tucking into mouth-watering *kouneli stifado*; I had been more than generous with the fresh thyme when preparing the dish. Beyond a cursory glance at the garlic chives which she decreed were in need of a good watering, Marigold was in no mood to loiter. She ignored my suggestion that it may be tactful to stop and smell the roses so to speak, to give Guzim and Luljeta a few moments alone to catch up.

"Don't be silly. They're stuck outside because I have his key," Marigold retorted, displaying an uncharacteristic eagerness to get up close with my gardener.

"They may not appreciate us barging in..." I persisted.

"Nonsense, Guzim will be over the moon when he sees what I've done to his shed. He won't be able to believe the complete transformation I have worked. I may have missed my calling; perhaps I should have been an interior decorator instead of a pet food taster. I can't wait for Barry and Vangelis to finish with all the boring flooring and plastering so that I can get my teeth stuck into the *apothiki*."

"Perhaps my mother would like to put her own stamp on it," I suggested.

"Nonsense, she'll be quite content as long as we buy her a decent chip pan."

Whipping out the key to the shed, Marigold switched to Greek as she bore down on Guzim, calling out that she had his key. "*Echo to kleidi sou.*"

Even though it was clear we were interrupting a private moment, Marigold steamrollered ahead regardless. Visible evidence of fresh tears lined Luljeta's face. It was impossible to determine if Guzim was attempting to comfort his wife or if he had been haranguing her. Despite Marigold's general propensity for matchmaking, she blithely interrupted; refusing to tolerate the notion that the Albanian shed dweller had feelings. The couple exchanged muttered words before Guzim announced that his wife didn't understand Greek.

"Well, the shed will speak for itself," Marigold said. Throwing the door open with great aplomb, she invited us inside to admire her decorating skills.

Guzim tentatively stepped inside, the three of us following. It was admittedly a bit of a feat to cram four of us in the shed at once: there was barely enough room to swing a cat now that Guzim's battered old furniture had been dragged back inside, albeit well hidden under vast swathes of our old curtain fabric.

Marigold had somehow managed to revamp Guzim's old iron bedstead; with a healthy dose of imagination it now a resembled a chic daybed. A garish psychedelic orange valance skirted its base, a mass of ruffled cushions piled atop what I recognised as Benjamin's old tartan sheets. It was a good job that I still had my sunglasses on to combat the riot of colour.

I found myself quite mesmerised by the cushions, the mix of fabrics offering a pictorial walk down the memory lane of the curtains which had lined our windows over the years. The bizarre hotchpotch of clashing colours used in the cushions was replicated in the multi-coloured rag rug, cobbled together by Doreen, now covering most of the bare concrete floor. Only the tell-tale electrical buzz identified the bulky oblong object concealed beneath what looked like an oversized table cloth matching the valance, as Guzim's old fridge.

The dented stainless steel sink which had lain on the floor on my previous visit, serving as a repository for old beer bottles, had now been plumbed in. Yet another frilly valance hung below the sink, no doubt concealing any old dented pots and pans. The old gas camping stove, scrubbed free of layers of grease, was now placed on a sturdy shelf, no longer posing the potential fire hazard it had before.

I suspected that Marigold had exploited Barry's good nature by forcing him to do the odd bit of plumbing and shelf fixing, in addition to slapping pink paint all over the formerly drab grey walls. She may even have called on his skill with electrics for the finishing touch: a string of fairy lights now replaced the old washing line which had been strung above the bed. I hoped that Guzim had enough electrical sense not to peg his wet socks to the twinkling display.

Breaking the prolonged silence, Marigold asked Guzim if he liked it, "*Sou aresei?*"

"*To roz,*" Guzim muttered in disbelief, staring in horror at the freshly painted pink walls. "*To roz einai to omofylofiliko chroma.*"

His observation that pink was a homosexual colour was mumbled: it was clear he was wary of antagonising Marigold.

"*Kai portokali,*" I added, pointing to the clashing orange features.

Clasping Guzim's hand tightly, Luljeta gazed around the shed, taking in all the details of her husband's abode, a look of wonder plastered on her face. I was unable to decipher a single word of the stream of Albanian she directed towards Guzim, but there was genuine awe in her voice when she switched to English.

"I cannot believe that Guzim lives in such a wonderful house, it is so big. It has much more room than our home in Albania."

Rather taken aback by her statement, I began to wonder if Luljeta's grasp of English was as proficient as I'd presumed. Their place in Albania housed seven of them when Guzim was home, yet she was proclaiming that Guzim's one room hovel was bigger than their Albanian dwelling. If her English was on point then it made the mind boggle about the sort of primitive and cramped conditions they were forced to endure in their native land.

"I know how proud Guzim is of owning his own home in Greece but he never told me it was so clean and comfortable. And so colourful."

"Well, to be fair, it was a bit of a pigsty until Marigold got her hands on it..." I began.

"I thought the place deserved a makeover in honour of your visit, dear," Marigold interrupted. "It really wasn't fit for female habitation before I got my hands on it. You know what slobs men can be when left to their own devices."

"I think you'll find that my efforts with the mop are more thorough than yours," I pointed out, offended by Marigold's gross generalisation of men as slobs. One does not have a long and illustrious career as a health inspector without maintaining the most exacting standards.

Completely ignoring me, my wife continued addressing Luljeta. "Barry, my brother, give the walls a nice lick of fresh paint. I thought that pink would give it a pretty feminine touch...it was a rather dingy grey before, not to mention horrendously grubby.   Oh, and my friend, Doreen, ran up that lovely valance for the bed."

"I don't know that word, valance..." Luljeta said.

"It's the frilly sheet that skirts the bed. It's a great way of hiding any bits and bobs; we hid most of Guzim's belongings under there. They were a bit of an eyesore."

"Belongings?" I questioned, unaware that Guzim had any possessions beyond the afore-mentioned old junk.

"Those shabby clothes that Guzim wears," Marigold explained.

"*Ti?*" Guzim grunted upon hearing his name mentioned. "*Ti?*"

"Oh yes, I almost forgot," Marigold said before addressing Guzim directly in painfully slow Greek, telling him that there were some new dresses for him under the bed. "*Yparchoun merika nea foremata yia esas kato apo to krevati.*"

"You mean *nea roucha*," I corrected my wife. "*Nea foremata* means new dresses."

"Victor, must you be so critical? I know what I mean. You know as well as I do that Greeks always refer to clothes as dresses."

"But Guzim is Albanian," I reminded her.

Firing a withering look in my direction, Marigold told Guzim that the new clothes were actually new, not second-hand, and had never been worn: "*Ta roucha einai kainourgia kai ochi apo deftero cheri. Den echoun forethi pote.*"

Guzim immediately threw himself on the rag rug in order to easily facilitate a good rummaging round under the bed. Grabbing hold of the spurned Christmas presents which Barry had gifted me, Guzim started spouting in guttural Albanian, clearly beyond excited to be the recipient of such largesse. It was hard to fathom that anyone could be so delighted to receive the brightly knitted Christmas pullover featuring the slogan 'Jingle', complete with immodestly placed bells, or the feather embellished 'Dirt Terminator' tee-shirt.

"What's he got there?" I asked Marigold, watching Guzim unfold a garish red number emblazoned with Christmas trees.

"It's that sleep suit that Barry bought you a few years back."

"What on earth was your brother thinking? It looks like an enormous babygrow," I shuddered. Even in bed, I insist on wearing a button down pyjama jacket rather than some nasty looking stretch number. Barry had clearly given little consideration to the issue of nocturnal visits to the lavatory when he opted for the tasteless all-in-one.

"*Einai kalo, einai poly poly kalo. Tha fanei poly kalo se afto,*" Guzim gushed, proclaiming the ghastly giant babygrow was very good. His assertion that he would look very good in it made me question his sanity. Guzim appeared so eager to prove the point that it would suit him that he started to discard the ragged clothes he was wearing, his hasty striptease act sending Marigold running out to the garden to spare her blushes. I hurried after her, having no desire to see Guzim prancing round in his underpants.

Guzim tripped out after us: to be precise he literally tripped over the too long trouser legs of the ridiculous sleep suit he had donned. His undignified exit from the shed left him sprawled on the ground, his face pressed up against an aubergine on the newly tacked up shower curtain. Throwing his arms around Marigold's shins, Guzim looked up at her, a devoted look on his face as he thanked her effusively for his wonderful new dresses.

"I notice that you didn't tell him that his

new clothes were actually my unwanted items," I peevishly pointed out as Guzim finally relinquished his hold on my wife's legs. I must confess to being a tad put out: his displays of grovelling prostration were usually directed towards me.

If I thought that Guzim looked a total fright in the Christmas tree bedecked babygrow, it was nothing to the grotesque image he presented when he squeezed his head through the Jingle pullover, rather rashly inviting Marigold to ring his bells.

"Well, he obviously appreciates the clothes but I must say his reaction to the shed makeover was a bit lacklustre..." Marigold began to say before her words were interrupted by Guzim unleashing a primeval scream of anguish.

Turning on Marigold in fury, Guzim demanded to know what she had done with his rabbit. *"Ti ekanes me tin Doruntina?"*

Marigold, unaccustomed to being screamed at by the lowly gardener, adopted an aggrieved tone of self-righteousness, telling him that if he was missing anything he must look in the bins: clearly she was unfamiliar with the pet name of Guzim's furry friend. Backing away from the enraged Albanian, Marigold hissed to me, "Why

has Guzim turned puce? We didn't sling anything of value in the rubbish."

"The missing Doruntina is his pet rabbit," I
explained. "You wouldn't like it if someone
threw your precious felines away like yesterday's trash."

"Don't be ridiculous, Victor. Of course I
didn't bin his rabbit nor did I give it to Kyria
Maria to skin for a casserole, though I must admit to being sorely tempted. She had the most
appealing recipe for cooking rabbit with raisins."

"So what did you do with it then?"

"It was completely unhygienic to keep a
rabbit hutch next to the bed, Victor. I would expect you more than anyone to agree."

"So what did you do with it," I pressed,
worried that Guzim was about to have an apo-
plectic fit.

"I put it out of the way behind the shower
curtain."

"*Ela Guzim, to kouneli sou,*" I said, pulling the
shower curtain to one side with a flourish to reveal Doruntina's cage. My big reveal fell a bit
flat since the rabbit hutch was concealed under
a garish orange cover sporting a soggy frilled
edge where the hosepipe had dripped. Since

Marigold and her sidekick had gone to such pains to envelop the hutch in an old curtain, it made me wonder if the pair of them had mistaken the rabbit for a budgie.

Ripping the cover to one side, Guzim joyously yelled, "*Den to skotose tote.*"

"Of course she didn't kill your rabbit. What kind of barbarian do you think my wife is?" I shouted, belatedly realising he couldn't understand me. Luljeta spared me the ordeal of translating my words into Greek by translating my English into Albanian. From her tone, I imagined that she was also chiding her husband for practically accusing my wife of going round murdering his bunny. Considering the circumstances, I made a mental note to avoid mentioning that we would be tucking into rabbit *stifado* as soon as our houseguests arrived.

Unlatching the hutch, Guzim pounced on his pet, showering the rather mangy looking creature with sloppy kisses: I have to say he treated it with more affection than I had noticed him bestow on his wife thus far. In addition to offering Marigold a grovelling apology, he changed his tune on the shed, declaring she had done a magnificent job of tidying it up. He may have slightly appeased my wife with his kowtowing grovelling, but his insincerity didn't fool me for a moment. I can't say I blame him: Marigold must have been out of her mind to expect a grown man to be grateful for having his seedy man cave transformed into a frilly pink palace.

On the bright side, Guzim did express his genuine approval of the new shower set up in glowing terms, proclaiming it would put an end to the old witch next door spying on him when he washed himself down under the hosepipe. His next words were spoken in Albanian to Luljeta: of course I can't say with any certainty but I could swear that Violet Burke's name cropped up. I wouldn't put it past the ungrateful wretch to be disparaging my mother's good name and accusing her of spying on him, along with Maria. It struck me that Guzim must have a deluded image of what he actually looks like when stripped down to his underpants.

Making what I think Guzim must imagine was the ultimate conciliatory gesture, he suddenly thrust Doruntina into the unwilling arms of my wife.

"Victor, tell him to get it away from me," Marigold screeched. "It was sleeping on a flea ridden blanket before Doreen made it some new bedding."

Wriggling free, the rabbit hopped off, Guzim following in hot pursuit before it could do any damage to my lettuces. As Marigold stalked back to the house, furiously scratching, I thought to myself *that should put an end to her meddling in other people's sheds.*

Chapter 13

Musical Bedrooms

Whilst Marigold disappeared to shower off any random rabbit fleas, I took the opportunity to flick through the pages of some of her glossy Greek cookbooks, seeking inspiration for potential cookery classes. Since winter would be fast approaching by the time I finished my temporary spell running the shop, I decided to look for dishes that would be suitably warming and could be concocted from seasonal local ingredients. I felt that the obvious classics of *moussaka* and *pastitsio* may present too much of a culinary challenge for an utter noob like Norman: after all, he had admitted he didn't even have a clue how to work the oven.

Although I would be sure to wow an audience by demonstrating my prowess in preparing *papoutsakia*, I considered that the béchamel sauce required for stuffed little shoes fashioned from aubergines may well lead to temper tantrums if my students' efforts turned out lumpy or burnt. I would need to wait until they were skilled enough to progress to advanced classes before introducing them to the finer points of classic sauces.

It struck me that the obvious solution was to begin by introducing them to one pot dishes such as winter stews. The recipe for rabbit with raisins, *kouneli me stafides*, sounded familiar: perchance it was the same one that Kyria Maria fancied making out of Doruntina. The instructions seemed straightforward enough for even a numbskull like Sherry to grasp, as long as she wasn't too squeamish when it came to dealing with entrails: the recipe was quite specific in calling for the use of a rabbit complete with said entrails. I reasoned that Giannis' rabbits would be plentiful since I doubted they were seasonal creatures and I knew from bitter, nay messy experience, that Giannis didn't bother to gut them. Moreover the recipe included thyme and garlic, thus offering my students the opportunity to experiment with herbs.

The glossy photograph of *kotopoulo me elies ke kokines piperies* caught my eye: the image of black olives and red peppers nestling next to the browned chicken was so striking that I could almost conjure the tempting aroma. I made a mental note to add it to my teaching repertoire if I decided to go ahead with the classes, though I hoped the selected dishes would not prove too ambitious. It could turn into a tedious chore if I had to begin with the absolute basics and show them what to do with an egg. At least the hens were laying well if it came to that.

My culinary browsing was disturbed when Marigold breezed in, carefully dressed to be sure to outshine Geraldine. She looked quite lovely despite the stubborn streak of pink paint standing out against her Titian tresses.

"What are you doing with those cookery books, dear? Are you planning on cooking up a feast for tomorrow evening?" Marigold asked.

"Just mulling a few dishes that I plan to experiment with over the winter," I said. I needed

to give more thought to the business of conducting cookery classes in our kitchen before
broaching the idea with my wife: women are
known to get quite territorial when it comes to
their kitchens. "If you're expecting me to cook
tomorrow, you're out of luck. I've got the trip
down to the Caves of Diros on Pegasus."

Marigold's brow furrowed in confusion. "I
thought that you were working in the shop
now."

"Tomorrow is my last boat trip of the season. I don't officially start at the shop until the
day after when Tina has to be at the hospital
with her mother."

"I could have sworn you were working in
the shop today…"

"I was there to get some on the job training,"
I said. Exasperated, I nevertheless resisted the
urge to tell my wife that sometimes I thought
she never listened to a word that I said. It
wouldn't do to needlessly introduce dishar-
mony to the Bucket household just before the arrival of houseguests.

"Since you're off on the boat tomorrow, perhaps we could turn it into a nice day trip out
with Geraldine and Ashley," Marigold suggested.

"Captain Vasos always says your family are welcome on Pegasus anytime."

"Geraldine and her sexually infected chap aren't family though," I protested rather peevishly, having no wish to be lumbered with entertaining them whilst I was working. "It wouldn't do to take liberties by expecting preferential treatment."

"You could always buy them tickets if you don't want to come across as a freeloader, dear."

"I've a feeling the trip is fully booked, you know how popular it is," I prevaricated. "Anyway, I doubt that your houseguests will want such an early start. I expect they might want to enjoy a lie in after the long drive today. It's certainly taking them long enough."

"Geraldine was always up early last time she stayed," Marigold persisted.

"That's because she was sneaking off to church for covert assignations with a certain cleric," I reminded her.

"Well, the less said about that the better. Best if we don't let that slip in front of Ashley."

"My lips are sealed," I promised. Escaping to the bathroom for a shower, I fervently hoped that Marigold had done a thorough job of washing any stray fleas down the drain. There is nothing more irritating than random fleas and mosquitoes taking advantage and biting one's intimate parts whilst one is naked and vulnerable to attack in the shower.

"I can't think where they've got to," Marigold said for the umpteenth time, moving aimlessly between the balcony and the kitchen. "The rabbit *stifado* will be over defrosted by the time they arrive."

"I'm not sure that's actually a thing," I replied, loading the last of the cutlery into the dumb waiter ready for the bucket on the rope to be hoisted up to the roof terrace when we dined. I turned to give my wife my undivided attention. Marigold was clearly antsy over the late arrival of her friend.

"Perhaps they've got lost," Marigold speculated, consulting her watch.

"That's not very likely. Geraldine has holidayed here twice before, she knows how to find us," I pointed out. "Why are they driving from Athens? Couldn't they get a Sunday flight to the local airport?"

"Oh really, Victor, sometimes I think you never listen to a word that I say. I told you that they flew to Athens because Ashley was very keen to visit some stuffy museum there."

Marigold's reply piqued my interest: per-haps Ashley wouldn't turn out to be some sci-ence bod bore after all if he went out of his way to appreciate the finer aspects of Athenian cul-ture.

"Which site was he keen to visit? The Acropolis Museum or the National Archaeolog-ical Museum."

I had very much enjoyed visiting both ven-ues on our occasional mini-breaks to the Greek capital, though Marigold was less keen, prefer-ring to drag me round the shopper's paradise of Plaka and Monastiraki. If it came to a toss up be-tween appreciating the cultural artefacts housed in the Benaki Museum or dawdling round Marks and Spencer, the latter won Marigold's vote every time.

"No, Geraldine said it was some rather dingy medical place that only opens a couple of mornings a week. She didn't fancy it but was go-ing along to keep Ashley happy."

I surmised that Geraldine's approach was much like my own, dutifully trotting along be-hind Marigold for yet another torturous trip to Marks and Sparks. I suppose in fairness, Mari-gold does humour me, accompanying me on my museum trips even though she would much prefer to spend her time flashing my credit card in the shops. On balance, over the course of our three plus decades together, we have managed to negotiate the give and take of marriage tolerably well.

"I just hope that Geraldine doesn't allow herself to become a doormat. You know how eager she always is to please whenever she has a new boyfriend," Marigold said, biting her lip nervously.

"Well, I certainly never had her down as a church goer until she took up with Andreas," I said.

"Do try to remember not to bring Andreas up in front of Ashley, he may be the jealous type," Marigold warned again.

"I would hope that Geraldine has been discreet," I said. "It wouldn't do at all for her to have been shouting it from the rooftops that she was meeting up with a supposedly celibate cleric."

"Geraldine was the soul of discretion and she never so much as hinted at any hanky panky between them," Marigold protested. Rushing to peer over the balcony, she cried out, "I can hear a car, perhaps this is them now. Oh, false alarm, it's only Spiros' hearse. I do hope there hasn't been a local death."

"Don't worry; Spiros is using the hearse to give Sampaguita driving lessons. The new bus service is impossible."

Meli had recently been added to the bus route to town, but the service proved rather impractical. The early morning bus was scheduled on Greek time, meaning it could turn up half an hour either side of its stated arrival time. There was only one return bus each day, landing in Meli early evening, though I suppose it was quite remarkable that the bus did manage to return on the same day.

"Ooh, this is them now. Come on, Victor, we must go down to greet them," Marigold cried excitedly, making a dash for the door. Dutifully following my wife downstairs, I watched as Geraldine practically hurled herself out of the hire car, smothering Marigold in an enthusiastic embrace. Geraldine's male companion appeared in no great rush to exit the car, making a point of folding a road map in neat and precise lines before fussily removing a pair of leather driving gloves. I assumed he could well be the shy type, anxious about meeting old friends of his girlfriend and making a good impression.

Bearing in mind that he may well feel awkward being the houseguest of total strangers, I made a mental note to make allowances for him.

Geraldine appeared in fine fettle as she rushed over to greet me. I noticed that she'd piled on a few pounds since her last visit to Greece, but the pleasantly plump look rather suited her. Perhaps it was an indication that she had indeed found contentment with this Ashley fellow.

"Now, I must introduce you both to Ashley," Geraldine declared, turning to face the car. A look of embarrassment flitted over her features when she realised that her new man was still seated behind the steering wheel, seemingly engrossed in jotting something down in a notepad. As Geraldine hovered on the pavement, her nervous movements putting me in mind of a scalded cat, he made no effort to step out of the car to join her.

"Ashley, what are you doing in there?" Her tone was wielding as she tentatively tapped his window as though afraid of annoying him. A note of false cheer inflected her voice as she desperately repeated his name, "Ashley."

Firing an irritated frown at his beloved, Geraldine's new chap carefully capped his pen before making a move to exit the car. I was rather taken aback as he unfurled himself from the vehicle, his lanky frame towering above Geraldine and giving my own six feet a run for their money. There was something about his gangly frame that put me in mind of Frankenstein's monster. I immediately hoped that the pavement formalities would not be long and drawn out: the sooner I could get him seated, the less chance there was of getting a crick in my neck.

"Ashley, these are my good friends, Marigold and Victor Bucket," Geraldine said by way of introduction. As Ashley turned to greet my wife, I found myself fixating on the rather unnatural sheen of his lush bouffant hair, precisely contoured around protruding and overly large ears. The early evening sun reflected the lustrous gloss of his dark brown hair, the rather unnatural looking colour standing out in marked contrast to his pasty white skin. For a moment I imagined the sheen of his hair had a tinge of nylon about it. I immediately dismissed the thought that his hair was too good to be true: it was just as likely that the gloss was down to Geraldine sharing her predilection for pet food with him, rather than him favouring an artificial thatch.

I recalled Marigold telling me that Geraldine's new chap was a good decade younger than her friend, but his rather stuffy manner belied the general image of a toy boy.

"It is so important to make a note of the exact mileage. One can't trust these car hire places to be accurate," Ashley said, fastidiously wiping one hand on his shorts before extending it in greeting. Despite the quick wipe, his hand was unpleasantly damp. His shorts skirted his knees, exposing only a narrow circle of chalky skin above his knee-length socks, held in place with a pair of old fashioned garter belt straps. I mentally conceded that Marigold may have a point when she constantly chuntered on about my combination of socks with sandals not being particularly stylish. Although I would never be caught dead in a pair of garters, I would definitely need to give some serious consideration to abandoning the habit of pairing my socks with sandals even if it was a pretty foolproof method of preventing mosquitoes from sucking the blood from my ankles.

"How was the journey from Athens?" I asked. "Did you make good time?"

"Our arrival time is precisely fifty-four minutes later than I calculated. Geraldine neglected to mention that she finds map reading rather challenging." I wasn't too surprised that Ashley's reedy voice mirrored his reedy appearance.

"I did my best, Ashley. It wasn't easy because the map was in Greek..."

"You did mention that more than once on the drive, nineteen times to be exact," Ashley retorted with unsmiling punctiliousness.

"Well, you're here now, that's all that matters," Marigold said cheerily. "Come upstairs and have a glass of wine."

"A cup of decaffeinated tea would be most welcome," Ashley stiffly replied. Following my wife up the stairs, he left Geraldine to lug all their bags up, his marked lack of chivalry leaving her flushed and embarrassed.

Naturally I stepped into the breach, almost giving myself a hernia as I attempted to lift the largest suitcase.

"Good grief, what have you got in here? A dead body?" I chortled.

"That's Ashley's case. I expect it's full of books. He's researching mould."

"Mould..."

"Or something that sounds like it. It's something very scientifically technical to do with Ashley's work."

By the time I had dragged Ashley's case up the stairs, I was more than a little winded. I imagined his case must be stuffed with every last tome on mould ever printed. Still, the intriguing subject of mould would certainly make for an interesting conversation over dinner; I find the huge variety of spores quite fascinating.

"I'll just pop these bags in the guest bedroom so that you can get settled," I offered.

"Lead the way. I'd like to get the unpacking out of the way before that cup of tea. I'm a great believer in a place for everything and everything in its place," Ashley pontificated.

"Geraldine, leave the unpacking until later and come and join me in a glass of wine," Marigold urged.

Casting a yearning glance at the glass of wine Marigold proffered, Geraldine dithered, clearly torn. "I should unpack first. Ashley does like things done properly. He's a great stickler for everything in its place."

I found Geraldine's deferment to Ashley rather telling. It was blatantly obvious that she was keen on him, even though in addition to being a bit of a cold fish, he was neither handsome nor well built: there again, he was single, which is Geraldine's primary requirement when hunting a potential husband.

As I showed the two of them into the guest bedroom, Geraldine giggled nervously and Ashley turned noticeably red, fussily decreeing, "Oh no, I'm afraid this won't do at all. Not at all."

"I prepared the room specially," Marigold said, understandably at a loss as to what he could possibly find to object to in our tastefully decorated guest bedroom, mercifully devoid of piles of clashing cushions. Frantically elbowing me out of the way, Marigold gave the room a thorough once over, a flummoxed look on her face. The room was inviting with not a thing out of place; Marigold had gone out of her way to ensure their comfort. Wondering if she had missed something, she adopted an apologetic tone. "I gave it a good mopping and aired the sheets outside."

Like Marigold, I was curious as to why Ashley found the room lacking. Perchance he had expected to find luxury chocolates on the pillow or a vase of freshly cut flowers by the bed. Such touches would be completely impractical: any chocolates left lying around would melt in the heat and leave a mess on the pillow and freshly cut flowers would encourage aphids to breed indoors.

"I don't doubt that you are a thorough hostess," Ashley said, his haughty tone managing to imply the opposite. "But this room only has a double bed; it certainly won't do at all. I have seen far too many abhorrent sights in my professional line of work to lightly entertain pre-marital congress. Geraldine and I have not yet reached the stage where we would be comfortable making a bedroom commitment."

Scooping Catastrophe up, Geraldine buried her face in its fur, using the cat to conveniently hide her blushes. It appeared that Ashley was still too engrossed in pontificating to hear his girlfriend mutter, "Speak for yourself."

Struggling to hold back my snort of laughter, I discreetly turned it into a cough. Geraldine really could pick them; it appeared that her latest boyfriend was no more inclined to enter into an amorous relationship than the celibate cleric she had ditched him for.

"Ashley, I will make up the sofa bed for you in Victor's office," Marigold offered, clearly flustered that her painstaking preparations had been found lacking. Following Marigold through to my office, Ashley looked rather put out that Geraldine would be having the superior room. When he had the bare faced temerity to suggest that perhaps he, rather than Geraldine, should take the guest room since the sofa bed was a bit on the short side considering his height, Marigold shot him down with one of her withering looks.

Less than overjoyed at the prospect of Ashley taking over my office, I did a quick scan of the room to ensure there was nothing lying about which could be incriminating. It wouldn't do at all for Ashley to discover my moving abroad manuscript and decide to amuse himself with a spot of bedtime reading. Fortunately, the book and my jottings for its sequel were securely locked away in my filing cabinet, well away from prying eyes. Ever mindful of being a good host, I selected a book on bacteria that I knew had a fascinating chapter on mould spores, thoughtfully leaving it in a handy spot on the bedside table for our guest.

"Geraldine, do take Ashley through to the kitchen for a glass of wine whilst we make up the sofa bed," Marigold urged when she returned with fresh linen. "Victor will give me a hand here."

"I really would prefer a cup of decaffeinated

tea," Ashley stated, reluctantly trailing after Geraldine.

"I'm a bit surprised that Geraldine didn't give me the heads up that they would need separate rooms rather than leaving it to the last moment to play musical bedrooms," Marigold complained.

"She did appear quite disappointed that they wouldn't be sharing a bed. I think it came as a surprise to her. I must confess to feeling a tad sorry for Geraldine. Either her new boyfriend is a bit of a prig or he simply does not reciprocate the besotted feelings she has spent countless hours bending your ear about," I hissed to my wife. The annoying thought struck me that my long distance telephone bill would most certainly be a testament to Geraldine's infatuated outpourings.

"I was thinking the same thing. From everything Geraldine told me, I thought she'd landed herself a hot-blooded toy boy, not some uptight prude," Marigold said as we tucked the bottom sheet in. Moving over to the door to make sure that Ashley wasn't lurking outside, Marigold whispered, "Even though he's in his late 40s, he has never been married. You don't suppose he could still be a virgin?"

"Just because he is in no great hurry to jump into bed with Geraldine, one can't rush to conclusions," I cautioned. "Perhaps he really is worried about picking up something nasty. She has been round the block a few times."

"Just because she's dated a lot doesn't mean she was promiscuous," Marigold said, plumping the pillow with unnecessary force. From the look on her face, I would hazard a guess that my wife was imagining the pillow was our rather ungracious guest.

"I didn't mean to imply that she was. I know what a disaster her love life has been, it's not as though you don't share all the excruciating details about her myriad failed relationships."

My words elicited a withering look from Marigold. "Victor, you know as well as I do that Geraldine just wants to find someone to settle down."

"And going by that tall drink of water she's dragged along it seems that she's not too fussy who with…"

"I wouldn't exactly describe him like that," Marigold snorted. "A tall drink of water usually refers to someone who is considered attractive."

"Oh, I thought it was an idiom for someone tall…"

"Tall and gorgeous," Marigold insisted. "You don't suppose that Ashley is just using Geraldine to get a free holiday?"

"I suppose it's a possibility. It will be easier to determine when we have had more chance to study them as a couple."

"I suppose I'd better go and make him that cup of tea."

"Decaffeinated," I reminded her.

"For goodness sake, does he think he's staying in a five star hotel? I'll have to give him that Greek stuff with the twigs in it."

"*Tsai tou vounou*," I reminded her. "Make mine a brandy. I've a feeling I'll need it."

Chapter 14

Getting up Victor's Nose

Marigold had set the scene for dinner on the roof terrace with such perfection that there was nothing for Ashley to find fault with, though it was not for want of trying. Although he had only been in our home for less than an hour, I felt that I had the measure of him, deducing that nit-picking was his speciality. Geraldine repeatedly emphasised that Ashley considered himself a perfectionist; personally, I find the term obsessively anal more fitting.

BUCKET TO GREECE (VOL. 8)

Earthenware pots housing Marigold's flowering plants were dotted around the terrace, our recently acquired hanging solar lanterns illuminating the vibrant petals of the floral blooms. The table was set with crisp white linen, not even loosely related to any old curtains: the dark blue crockery, against the white backdrop, was deliberately chosen to emphasise Greek themed al fresco dining. Although it was too dark for our guests to appreciate the magnificent view, the sky above us was a star-gazer's paradise, free of the light pollution they were used to back in Manchester.

I was delighted that it was still warm enough in the evenings to dine outside. I particularly welcomed the fresh autumn breeze, negating as it did the overpowering stench of TCP disinfectant emanating from Ashley's hairline. He had made such a fuss, when, during the course of unpacking he placed some of his weighty books on the newly erected shelf in my office, sending the whole thing toppling down on his head. The ensuing cut, although admittedly bloody at the time, was barely discernible now. Fortunately, Ashley's long standing apprehension of foreign needles spared me the ordeal of driving him down to the clinic to be stitched up.

"Victor always bodges any DIY he attempts," Geraldine informed Ashley.

"I did tell him to get Barry round to do it, but would he listen?" Marigold volunteered as we tucked into our appetiser of *salata karota trimeno me agouri*. I find that this simple salad of grated carrots and cucumbers sounds much fancier when one introduces it to the table by its Greek name.

"Here Geraldine, have another drop of wine," I offered, slopping some cheap plonk from a plastic bottle into her glass in the hope that it would shut her up. Considering it rather ill-mannered of Geraldine to keep harping on about my inability to fix a shelf to a wall without it almost turning into involuntary manslaughter, I was glad that I hadn't wasted my money by opening a bottle of the good stuff from Lidl. I could hardly have been expected to know that my superglued shelf would be expected to bear the weight of every tome on mould ever penned.

"I don't suppose you happen to know if these carrots are organic," Ashley asked.

"Of course I know. I grew them myself."

"I tried growing my own but for some reason they didn't germinate. It may have been down to the lack of sunshine in my bathroom," Ashley said.

"You tried to grow carrots in your bathroom. How bizarre," Marigold scoffed.

"I resorted to what you consider bizarre methods since I live in a third floor apartment and I don't have a garden. I did consider an allotment but when I enquired I was told there were over 500 people on the waiting list."

"Geraldine has a garden, it's compact but I'm sure there's enough room for you to plant a few carrots," Marigold suggested, unable to resist a bit of meddling.

"Indeed, Geraldine does have a garden the size of a postage stamp but formal documents may need to be drawn up before I could even consider planting in it," Ashley said.

"You don't get many carrots with an official contract affixed," I pointed out. "I prefer mine with a bit of leafy foliage."

"If we discover we are not compatible, the question may arise of who any sprouted carrots legally belong to." Pausing to inspect a hunk of Dina's homemade bread before dipping it in olive oil, Ashley continued, "Geraldine could attempt to assume custody of said carrots as it is her land."

"Ah, so you're thinking of something along the lines of a pre-sprouting carrot agreement," I snorted.

"You may mock, Victor, but an awful lot of digging and watering could go to waste in the event of a relationship breakdown," Ashley said. With his nostrils flaring, there was no denying that Ashley looked down his nose when he spoke to me. I don't recall if I mentioned that Ashley has abnormally large nostrils, without doubt the most enormous ones I have ever seen: you could easily shove a banana up his hooter with plenty of room to spare.

"Victor, would you give me a hand dishing up the rab...with the chicken *stifado*?" Marigold requested once the salad course was dispensed with.

"Certainly, dear. I'll be right down as soon as I've loaded the salad plates into the dumb waiter."

"You want to make sure that there's no one on the pavement below before you load anything into that bucket," Geraldine giggled. "Marigold warned me that you designed it yourself."

"Well, thus far any passing pedestrians have

been spared a killer blow from my bucket," I retorted.

"Yes, but Papas Andreas did end up with the dregs of a bottle of wine all over his cassock when you unfurled the rope a bit too quickly," Marigold said.

"I think you will find that the technical name is a *kalimavkion* rather than a cassock..." I abruptly stopped mid-sentence, brought up short by the sight of Marigold's hands flying up to cover her gaping mouth. Despite her repeated warnings not to mention Papas Andreas in front of Ashley, Marigold had been the one to go and put her foot in it. Fortunately, Ashley was too preoccupied with trying to prise a piece of carrot loose from a back molar to notice Geraldine's blushes.

"It doesn't look very encouraging," Marigold sighed as soon as we were alone in the kitchen. "Geraldine seems much keener than him."

"Indeed. One can't fail to notice that Ashley seems to go out of his way to voice his doubts about their relationship going anywhere," I agreed.

"Perhaps he's just being cautious. The way he was going on about the legalese of carrot

ownership put me in mind of pre-marital arrangements."

"You could be right. If he has a pre-marital
contract on his mind he may be considering pro-
posing but protecting his interests. Perchance
he's just very old fashioned and doesn't want to
jump into bed before marriage," I suggested.
"How can I say this without sounding crude? It
wouldn't appeal to me to buy the goods without
sampling them first, if you get my drift."

"It was your sampling of my goods that
meant we had to get married because Benjamin
was on the way," Marigold reminded me, hur-
riedly adding, "But of course I would have married you anyway. For all we know, Ashley may
have suffered a tumultuous breakup in the past
and is simply protecting his heart by moving
slowly with Geraldine. Maybe he'll loosen up
after a drop more wine."

"I think Geraldine may have plans to get
him tipsy and lure him into the guest bedroom.
Have you seen the way she keeps topping up his
glass?"

"Best bring another couple of bottles up
with the *stifado* then," Marigold winked.

"I hear that you raise your own chickens," Ashley said, scrutinising the piece of rabbit on his fork before popping it into his mouth.

"With a little help from Guzim, my Albanian gardener."

"Well, I must say this chicken is excellent. I assume that we are eating one of your own brood," Ashley praised as he chewed away on his rabbit, completely oblivious to what he was actually eating. "There's nothing quite like eating organically raised chicken when one is intimately familiar with the source."

"I'm afraid you assume wrongly..." I began to say.

"Victor won't hear of us eating his pet chickens, he's most particular on that point. I expect that this chicken came from Lidl," Marigold interrupted, desperate to keep up the pretence that we weren't tucking into a local bunny after having convinced herself that our guests would be overly squeamish if the truth came out.

"What a strange attitude to have. One really shouldn't go getting attached to livestock; it ought to be raised as food," Ashley pronounced.

"I take it that you must have a wealth of experience raising a clutch of chickens in your third floor bathroom." Even though my voice was laden with sarcasm, my comment did not elicit one of Marigold's withering looks. She had gone clean off the idea of chucking Raki in the cooking pot when I pointed out that in the event of her murdering my favourite chicken, she would personally have to pluck it and gut it as I would have nothing to do with it.

Ashley's only response was a visible flare of his enormous nostrils.

Chapter 15

Mould and Moulage

Realising that it could become more than a jot awkward giving house room to Ashley if the dinner descended into complete acrimony, I resolved to rescue the situation by playing up my role of good host. With an early morning start on Pegasus looming, I had to refrain from knocking back the wine; nevertheless I topped up his glass and steered the conversation around to our common interest.

"I hear that you are something of an authority

on mould, Ashley," I flattered him. "I too find the many types of fungal microorganisms most engrossing."

"I've never had the slightest interest in the subject," he responded as though the fascinating subject was beneath him. I imagined that the blank look in his eyes combined with his marked pallor accentuated by the solar lanterns, made his resemblance to a dead fish on a slab quite remarkable.

"But Geraldine told me that you find mould quite enthralling…"

"I can't think why she would get such a pre-posterous notion in her head," Ashley said as though Geraldine wasn't seated right beside him tucking into *kouneli stifado.* "I shudder to think how anyone could anyone find mould in-teresting?"

"Well, I do actually…very much so in fact."

"It's always been a mystery to me why Vic-tor finds such a dull topic so riveting. Person-ally, I find the subject most off-putting, espe-cially whilst I'm eating. If Victor insists on bringing mould up at the table, I find myself in-specting my food for suspicious growths," Mar-igold piped up. Ignoring the withering look I fired in her direction for siding with the enemy, she adroitly changed the subject.

"Did you enjoy your stay in Athens? It is such a beautiful city."

"Yes, indeed. I was keen to go to Athens since there is a one of a kind museum there which I wanted to visit…"

Marigold interrupted Ashley, no doubt desperate to stop him before he could start rambling on about another topic she found as tedious as mould. "Geraldine, did you manage to get to the Parthenon this time?"

"Oh yes, we went up yesterday afternoon," Geraldine said. "The museum Ashley wanted to visit wasn't open until this morning so I managed to persuade him to make the hike up there."

"And did the Parthenon meet with your approval?" I asked Ashley. Although I attempted to temper the sarcasm in my voice, I expected him to find fault with something, be it the scaffolding at the famous site or the presence of too many other tourists.

"I found it an impressive site indeed, such grandeur," Ashley said. "One could feel a real sense of history."

Geraldine beamed so proudly upon hearing Ashley praise the Parthenon that one could be forgiven for thinking that she'd personally had a hand in its construction.

"And did you manage to get to Plaka, too?" Marigold asked. Before they had the chance to reply, Marigold immediately butted back in, offering her two penn'orth worth. "I just love the ambiance of the Plaka quarter. There are so many delightful places to dine on Mnisikleous Street."

In response to Ashley's questioning raised eyebrow, I told him, "That's the famous Plaka staircase street you see in all the postcards, the one lined with cafes and restaurants…"

"Such an atmosphere," Marigold interrupted. "We do so love to enjoy a *mezedes* in one of the quaint Greek restaurants there. Such a wonderful selection of eateries to choose from, isn't there, Victor?"

"Indeed there are, though I believe that none of them quite compare to our humble local taverna here in Meli. We are so lucky to have the freshest food on our doorstep and of course the prices in Plaka are a total rip-off in comparison."

"Victor couldn't believe his luck to discover our local taverna is the cheapest in Greece. The prices are right out of the last century," Marigold said.

"Which is amazing in itself when one considers one usually pays the premium of an arm and a leg for quality organic ingredients," I pointed out.

"Organic, you say. I'd be interested in sampling the food there one evening," Ashley said with something close to enthusiasm.

"I'm not sure it's really your thing, Ashley," Geraldine cautioned, a wary look on her face. "It's probably a bit too spit and sawdust for your taste. The owner is very lax about keeping the place spotless."

"Surely you must be mistaken," Ashley contradicted. "You told me that Victor used to be a public health inspector back in Manchester. I find it difficult to credit that he would sing the praises of any establishment with less than exacting hygiene standards."

"The general air of grubbiness is mainly superficial. I make allowances because of the superb quality of the food and the warm welcome we receive," I said in defence of my favourite haunt.

"And we've never once come down with a nasty case of food poisoning after eating there," Marigold added before hastily changing the subject. "Victor, perhaps we should follow

Geraldine and Ashley's example and have another break in Athens soon."

"Mini-breaks don't grow on trees," I reminded her.

"But the trip could pay for itself, dear," Marigold wheedled.

"How so?"

"Barry was telling me that you were thinking of having a car boot sale to get rid of the junk from the *apothiki*. For all we know, some of the knick knacks that we inherited along with the house from the previous owner may be worth a bob or two. With your experience of selling on the market, you could probably flog the lot at the flea market in Monastiraki," Marigold suggested.

"Was the previous owner the poor man that plunged to his death from your roof terrace?" Geraldine asked.

"It wasn't our roof terrace when he plunged from it," I protested. Ashley instantly shuffled his chair closer to the table, warily eyeing the distance between himself and the edge of the terrace. Spotting the look of panic on his face, I hastened to reassure him. "There weren't any ornamental railings around it at the time."

"So what do you think, Victor?" Marigold

nudged me.

"I think I have no intention of driving all the way to Athens with a Punto full of old junk. Can you imagine the amount of Greek bureaucracy involved in getting the necessary permit to sell things at the flea market? It would be much simpler to go along with Barry's idea of a local car boot sale."

"But I was thinking that Barry could come along to Athens too…"

"You know as well as I do that Barry loathes long distance car journeys due to his propensity for travel sickness. Come to think of it, he isn't too keen on cities either."

"That was before you told him all about the specialist tripe restaurants in Athens. What did you call them again?

"Pastsazidiko."

"That's it. Ever since you mentioned them, Barry has been keen to sample a bowl of trotter and tripe soup in an authentic *pastsazidiko*…"

"I'd rather we didn't talk tripe at the dinner table," Ashley interrupted. "I have a bit of a delicate stomach."

"So do tell us about the museum you visited," I urged. Whilst Marigold may find museum talk a tad boring, I hoped it might take her mind off expensive mini-breaks: my credit card was taking enough of a pummelling with the *apothiki* conversion to pay for.

"I'll just clear these plates and slice the watermelon for dessert," Marigold said, jumping up. "I can manage fine, Victor, you relax and enjoy the museum chat."

"The museum visit was everything I hoped for and more. Completely fascinating," Ashley said as Marigold rushed downstairs.

"Which museum was it? I don't think you mentioned it."

"The Wax Museum of Andreas Syggros," Ashley said in a tone that implied only a complete numbskull could fail to be familiar with the venue.

"Hmm, so that would be *To Mouseio Kerion tou Andrea Syngrou* in Greek," I said, showing off my knowledge of the Greek language whilst scrambling my brains as I tried to recall the museum. Drawing a blank, I admitted, "I must confess, I haven't heard of it. Is it a Greek version of Madam Tussauds? They really can create the most amazing likenesses these days."

"Oh no, you've got totally the wrong end of the stick. The Andreas Syggros Museum is quite a unique find. Whilst there are similar exhibits in Paris and Zurich, the Athenian one is acclaimed as the largest collection of moulage dedicated to the subject..."

"Moulage," I repeated. I was beginning to sense that Geraldine must have confused Ashley's interest in wax moulds with mould of the furry growth kind: I suppose for the uninitiated, not to mention disinterested girlfriends who only feign interest to butter their boyfriends up, it is easily done. For those not in the know, moulage refers to the casting of wax moulds to replicate wounds, primarily for the purpose of medical training. Of course, with the advent of modern technological advances such methods have now fallen into obscurity.

"Yes, moulage. If you're interested in paying it a visit, Victor, the actual museum is located in the Andreas Syggros Hospital of Cutaneous and Venereal Diseases. The wax models capture the most amazing array of deformities demonstrated by patients afflicted with venereal diseases."

I shuddered involuntarily, unable to believe that I was hosting a man tactless enough to dare to bring up the unseemly subject of venereal disease at my dinner table, a man moreover who claimed to be so sensitive that he couldn't even stomach a discussion about tripe. The very mention of unmentionable VD was enough to send my mind spinning down the unpleasant memory lane of being abandoned in a bucket and the subsequent indignity of being labelled V.D. Bucket, with all its unsavoury disease ridden connotations. I am generally spared such impromptu references to venereal disease these days since the term has rather fallen out of fashion, the promiscuous being more inclined to catch sexually transmitted infections in the modern era. Ashley's causal mention of the subject set my teeth on edge.

Considering that Marigold had told us that Ashley's job involved studying samples of sexually transmitted infections in a laboratory, it struck me that he must be going out of his way to deliberately rile me by dredging up such outdated vernacular. About to give him a piece of my mind, I stopped short. Ashley must surely be ignorant about the unfortunate initials I had been saddled with after the abandoned in a bucket debacle. Marigold would never have betrayed my confidence by blabbing to Geraldine; she would worry it would make her a laughing stock. Perchance our puffed-up house guest really did find the subject fascinating. With a clearly inflated idea of his own self-importance, I supposed he pretentiously used the old fashioned language in a desperate ploy to come across as more learned than he actually was. In all our years of marriage, Marigold has never once outed my original identity and she would never live it down if it came out now. Only Barry, Benjamin and Violet Burke are in on the secret.

"The wax depictions of pustular lesions in patients with gonorrhoea, not to mention the syphilitic chancres..." Ashley said, oblivious to how close he had come to having his head shoved into the leftover *stifado* put to one side for Pickles.

"Is a chancre the same as a canker?" Geraldine interrupted.

"Not unless the patient has been having unnatural congress with a fruit tree infected with fungal rot," Ashley said, his abnormally large nostrils flaring as he sarcastically schooled her.

"Or picked up something nasty from a dog that has an ear infected with parasitic mites," I volunteered, happy to steer the conversation away from what I considered the taboo subject of VD.

"The precision of detail on some of the anatomical limbs was extraordinary…" Ashley continued, only pausing for breath when Marigold returned with a platter of watermelon chunks.

"What have I missed? Anything exciting?" Marigold asked.

"I was just telling Victor about the anatomical limbs depicting the symptoms of VD," Ashley said.

"What?" Marigold spluttered, visibly paling when the too close to home reference to VD spewed from Ashley's mouth. Marigold is nothing if not sensitive to my original initials being used in a diseased context.

"Venereal diseases. I consider the wax models in the museum we visited to be nothing short of dermatological iconography," Ashley said, sounding as though he was regurgitating something he had picked up from a guidebook. "Now if you'll excuse me a moment, I must pay a visit to the little boy's room."

The moment he left the roof terrace, Geraldine took an enormous swig of wine before confiding, "I've never seen such grotesqueries in all my life. I tell you, I had a terrible job keeping my breakfast down; I never could have imagined anything as hideous as the things that I saw in that museum, such mangled monstrous horrors.

The whole experience was so morbid that I expect I will suffer from nightmares."

"So it wasn't really your cup of tea?"

"Well, naturally I feigned an interest," Geraldine admitted. "I read that it's important to be able to show an interest in things pertaining to one's partner's career."

"I found it much easier to just tune out when Victor used to witter on about hygiene violations and bacteria," Marigold said. "I found that it kept Victor happy if I just nodded along every now and again."

"I suppose you know best, Marigold. After all you've got the perfect marriage," Geraldine sighed.

"That's one way of describing it," Marigold snorted, filling up Geraldine's glass as Ashley returned. Unbelievably, he immediately carried on talking about VD as though the conversation was stuck in a time warp.

"They used the moulage as aids in the teaching of Dermatology and Aphrodisiology…"

I suppressed a snort of my own as I overheard Marigold whisper to Geraldine, "Like I said, it's best to just tune out. At least when Victor drones on, he does it in English. I can't make head or tail of what Ashley is on about."

"Me neither. I thought he loved anything mouldy," Geraldine hissed back.

"Such a pity that one has to leave England to appreciate the finer details of moulage," Ashley continued, sending a withering look in Geraldine's direction for failing to nod along robotically as he pontificated. "There's been nothing like it since The Society for the Suppression of Vice demanded that the models depicting venereal disease in Khan's Museum in London were destroyed. That was back in the Victorian era; you know what prudes those Victorians could be."

The involuntary snicker I emitted refused to be suppressed. The irony of a man too priggish to share a bedroom with his girlfriend lambasting something as prudish was just too delicious. Ashley, too caught up in the sound of his own voice to notice my derisory guffaw, continued apace.

"Still, I find it preposterous that they considered the models to be obscene and filthy rather than appreciating their value as tools of instruction. Such models could be used to enlighten the lower orders with loose morals about the dangers of engaging in the sort of depraved carnal activity that leads to disfiguring diseases."

"Fancy there being a Society for the Suppression of Vice in London," Marigold chuckled. "I wonder if they carried on like the Religious Police in Saudi Arabia. They're called something else...what is it, Victor?"

"The Committee for the Promotion of Virtue and the Prevention of Vice," I volunteered.

"Most likely the Saudis would have taken a more lenient approach than the Victorians," Ashley opined. "I expect they would have simply slung a bag over the heads of the models rather than destroying the figures as obscene."

"Indeed, some cultures consider an uncovered head to be more salacious than the naked body," I found myself agreeing.

"Do they even have such a thing as sexually transmitted infections in Saudi Arabia, what with the sexes being segregated and all that?" Geraldine slurred in a tipsy voice.

"How naïve you sound, Geraldine. There is immorality and depravity everywhere. Remind me to dig out the statistics on incidences of non-gonococcal urethritis in the Kingdom for you when we get back home. Of course, I'm not saying that venereal disease is as rampant there as it is Manchester, not unless the Arabs are fudging their figures. The way the Mancunian youngsters carry on these days is shocking; you'd think that they'd never heard of abstinence."

"Well, at least it must keep you busy analysing all those nasty samples," Marigold said.

"Oh it does," Geraldine agreed. "Only last week Ashley stood me up because he had a nasty dose of syphilis under his microscope. I'd done a nice cauliflower cheese for supper too, even going out of my way to make sure that the cauliflower was organic. The sauce had curdled by the next evening when Ashley finally turned up."

I winced at her words, knowing that I would never be able to look a cauliflower cheese in the floret again without mentally associating it with syphilis. It would be hard to shake the notion that syphilitic samples bore an uncanny resemblance to curdled cheese.

"I have apologised for that, Geraldine," Ashley said in a tone that implied his apology had been unnecessary. "But really, your curdled sauce is of no importance compared to the necessity of my tracking and tracing everyone who had sexual contact with a certain male stripper.

I am of the opinion that syphilitic outbreaks are the first sign of a society's moral collapse."

Marigold sent me a sympathetic look whilst simultaneously rolling her eyes. My wife knows me well enough to recognise that I had reached my limits of being lectured at by the insufferable bore. Oblivious to the air of disinterest around the table, Ashley continued to hold forth on his favourite subject until the arrival of Pickles put a sock in his verbal diarrhoea.

With nary a thought to polite table manners, Pickles sprang on top of the table, immediately sticking his tongue in the puddle of watermelon juice surrounding the remaining chunks of fruit, nosily slurping the liquid.

"What on earth is that disgusting creature doing on the table?" Ashley cried, brusquely taking matters into his own hands in an imperious fashion by jumping up and grabbing hold of the cat and slinging it to the ground. Whilst Marigold would certainly never encourage any of her felines to behave in such an uncouth manner, I could sense her outrage at Ashley's callous treatment of Pickles. No one messes with Marigold's pampered imported domestics or their spawn.

"If you wish to remain as a guest under this

roof, Ashley, I would suggest that you refrain from manhandling the felines in future," Marigold said, her steely tone brooking no argument.

"I'm sure he didn't mean to overreact, did you Ashley?" Geraldine said apologetically. "He's not really a cat person; they don't allow pets on the third floor."

Realising that he had overstepped the mark, Ashley stared at the ground as he muttered an apology. Finding it immensely satisfying to see Marigold take him down a peg or two, I made a mental note to treat Pickles to a tin of sardines the next morning. Alas, even though Ashley had been put in his place, he returned to his seat, helping himself to another glass of wine. I had rather expected that Marigold's dressing down would have encouraged him to retire for the night. I certainly wished that I could escape his company.

Settling for the next best thing, I put some distance between us by tidying up the almost empty bottles of plonk and loading them into the dumb waiter. As the bucket made its descent towards the kitchen window the peace of the evening was disturbed by a volley of Greek expletives from the street below. Peering over the

ornamental railings, I noticed the bucket swing-
ing in a precarious fashion, cringing when I
spotted Papas Andreas removing his stovepipe
hat. It appeared that the dregs from the wine
bottles must have landed on his head.

"*Sygnomi, Andrea.*" Shouting down an apology, I was relieved when Andreas responded
with a suitable quip that he saw it was raining
wine again: "*Vlepo oti vrechei xana krasi.*"

"Hold on a moment, Andrea. I have something for you, I'll bring it down," I called out before offering an insincere apology to our guests
for having to pop out on a bit of business.

As I rushed downstairs to grab the bag of
icons from my office, Marigold clattered after
me. Expecting to receive a lecture about my appalling rudeness in deserting the dinner party, I
was surprised to hear my wife tell me that she
wished she could make her escape too.

"I could tell that if you didn't get out from
under Ashley's feet for a moment that you
wouldn't be responsible for your actions, dear. I
was certainly tempted to clobber him when he
dared to touch Pickles."

"Geraldine certainly has a knack of picking
unsuitable men."

"I will try and prise her away from him tomorrow and find out if she really likes him or if she's just clinging on out of desperation and fear of being left on the shelf," Marigold said. "If she really does see a future with him, we must bite the bullet and try to get on with him."

All the irritation stoked by Ashley's company evaporated when I heard Marigold express such practical sense. It certainly brought home to me that I was a lucky man indeed to have such a wonderful wife, not to mention that the joy of being married spared me from the turbulent minefield of the dating game.

"I hope that Geraldine appreciates what a good and loyal friend you are," I said planting a kiss on Marigold's blushing cheek. "I certainly lucked out when I married you."

"I got lucky too," Marigold replied, bestowing a soft kiss on my lips.

"I'm off to get rid of those icons now. Don't wait up, darling. I may take a stroll through the village until our houseguest has gone to bed."

Chapter 16

Always Room for Loukoumades

Papas Andreas was waiting for me in the open doorway of his mother's house when I reached the street, clutching my Lidl carrier bag of Greek icons. As I sidestepped the puddle of spilt wine to prevent my socks from getting soggy, the esteemed cleric invited me in, *"Ela mesa."* Once indoors, he called out to Kyria Maria that they had a visitor, *"Mama, echoume enan episkepti."*

Andreas ushered me through to the kitchen where the black clad figure of his elderly mother hovered over the old fashioned cast iron wood-fuelled stove. As soon as the polite formalities were dispensed with, Kyria Maria immediately decreed that I looked in need of a good feeding up, making a beeline for the oven. The notion that I need feeding up is a constant refrain of my rail-thin octogenarian neighbour, a notion universally shared by every elderly Greek woman of my acquaintance.

"*Echo ligo pastitsio*," Maria insisted, lifting an enormous tray of the traditional baked pasta dish out of the oven.

"*Ochi, efcharisto. Den echo choro yia pastitsio, molis efaga ena megalo yevma*," I refused, telling her that I had no room left for *pastitsio* as I had just eaten a large meal.

Naturally that wasn't the end of the matter; refusing food in a Greek household is never that simple.

"*Ti efages*?" Maria demanded to know what I had eaten. I didn't for one moment doubt that she had anything but a genuine interest in my reply. My neighbour, along with most of the other villagers, was not backward about coming forward in her questions. Living in Meli, one must always be prepared to be grilled about every last morsel that had passed one's lips, along with a full disclosure of the cost of any new purchases and a summary of the balance in one's savings account. As a naturally reserved Englishman, albeit one of European citizenship with Greek residency, I had found it a bit of a culture shock to find myself bombarded with such personal questions when we first made the move to Greece.

"*Proti salata karota trimeno me agouri kai meta kouneli stifado. Yia na teleioso, eicha karpouzi,*" I replied dutifully telling her that our three-course meal had comprised salad, rabbit *stifado* and watermelon.

"*Kouneli. Sou afise o Alvanos na mageirepsei to kouneli tou?*"

I look of peevish envy flitted over Maria's face as she asked me if the Albanian had let me cook his rabbit. Fortunately I was spared the effort of scouring my brain for the appropriate Greek vocabulary to furnish an answer since Andreas responded on my behalf, telling his mother that Guzim would no more allow me to cook his pet than Maria would allow me to cook her pet tortoise.

Evidently relieved that I hadn't been given first dibs on the rabbit which she coveted for her own cooking pot, Maria once again tried to persuade me to have just a little pastitsio, "*Apla ligo pastitsio.*"

Maria could persist in her entreaties as much as she liked but I was determined to resist. I had no wish to overindulge, knowing the consequence would be a restless and uncomfortable night spent glugging Gaviscon directly from the bottle. I still suffer from humiliating flashbacks whenever I am reminded of the occasion when I had stuffed myself with her spaghetti and meatballs. Finally admitting defeat on the *pastitsio* front, Maria declared she would fry up a nice batch of *loukoumades* for Andreas and me.

Since a refusal would be pointless, I graciously accepted. I could never resist a serving of Maria's quite exquisite honeyed doughnuts. I reasoned that if I loosened my belt, I was sure I could make room for some of her irresistibly fluffy balls; after all, they are hollow. Maria often put temptation in my way by offering up a batch of the delicious sweet treats over the garden wall. I hadn't bothered mastering the cooking technique because in spite of her sweet tooth, Marigold had put her foot down and banned me from making *loukoumades* at home, convinced that the pair of us would pile on too many unwanted kilos to ever walk off. I briefly pondered the viability of skirting Marigold's ban by adding *loukoumades* to the range of dishes I would teach in my cookery classes. It struck me that such a move may be a tad risky; my potential pupils were not the sort to be trusted with a vat of boiling oil.

Maria had a batch of dough already prepared, no doubt on the off-chance someone might pop by in desperate need of feeding up on sweet dumplings. As she heated the oil and scooped the dough into teaspoon sized balls, I recalled the purpose of my visit. Turning to Andreas, I told him that I had something for him, *"Echo kati yia sena."*

"Ti einai afto?" My mind went blank when Andreas asked me what it was, the Greek word for icons completely eluding me. I really should have taken the time to consult my trusty English to Greek dictionary before stomping out of the house instead of relying on my ability to dredge up supposedly memorised words.

"Einai…einai ekosara," I said hesitantly, making a stab of a guess, plucking some random Greek word from the dark recesses of my brain and hoping it fitted.

A twinkle of amusement appeared in Andreas' eyes. *"Echeis eikosi chronon gynaika yia mena."*

Since Andreas had just said, "You have a twenty-year-old woman for me," I was rather taken aback, a tad alarmed that the Papas may mistake me for some kind of pimp. I'm sure the church must frown on foreigners going around offering young women to their clerics. Considering the potential magnitude of my latest language faux pas, I decided it would be safer to continue the conversation in English.

"There's been a terrible misunderstanding, Andrea. I don't have any young women for you."

"Not even the one I see to go in the shed of the Guzim?" he asked, his eyes still dancing in amusement.

"Certainly not. What I do have is a bag of old icons. Here, let me show you," I said, dipping into the Lidl carrier bag. "Perhaps some of them may be of special significance or even valuable."

"In the Greek the icon is the *eikonida*, not the *ekosara*," Andreas chuckled. "I think you to try to give me the woman what I see to go in the Guzim shed."

"That was Guzim's wife, Luljeta."

"Strange, she look the normal…"

"She is. It was something of a shock, I can

tell you. I'd imagined someone as shabby and toothless as Guzim. She actually seems very nice. If you have a chat with her over the garden wall, you'll need to speak to her in English as she doesn't understand Greek."

Andreas had been keeping up a running translation of our conversation in Greek for the benefit of his mother. I laughed out loud when Maria demanded to know how Luljeta could communicate with her husband if she didn't speak Greek. Andreas duly explained that the Albanian shed dweller's wife was Albanian, "*Einai Alvaniki, Mama.*"

I speculated that Andreas may be a rather disappointed to be palmed off with a bag of icons after I had built his hopes up on the female front. Since he didn't appear to be overly excited by the contents of the Lidl bag he was rummaging through, I threw caution to the wind, breaking the news that Geraldine was visiting. The emotive expression flitting over his features indicated that he was moved by my news. Realising there was no point in telling him only half a tale, I added that Geraldine's new boyfriend was with her.

"Does he to make her the happy?" Andreas asked in a low voice, not bothering to translate for his mother's benefit.

"I don't think he does. If I'm honest, he's a bit of a prig."

"Prig. I not to the understand…"

"*Einai ithikologos,*" I said, confident in my word choice this time as I had recently looked up the translation of prig to describe smug Bessie from the book club to Spiros. To hone the point, I added that Ashley was a prude, "*Einai damaskino.*"

Andreas' howl of laughter broke the tension. Belatedly realising that I had stupidly labelled Ashley a prune rather than a prude, I quickly corrected myself, "*Einai semnotyfos.*"

"I think this not to suit the Geraldine. She need the man with the passion," Andreas muttered, as though thinking aloud.

Abruptly changing the subject in an effort to conceal his emotions, Andreas studied an icon depicting a distinctly orange hued Jesus, wearing a solemn expression and what looked like a rather badly fitting wig.

"*Iisous Christos o Pantokratoras,*" he said, naming the figure in Greek.

"Is it valuable?"

Andreas tilted his head back and clucked his tongue in the non-verbal Greek way of saying no. I recognised the next painted icon that Andreas pulled from the bag: an identical copy of the gaudy reproduction depicting our Lady of the Sign, Platytera, conveniently disguises the unsightly fuse box in my hallway.

"These *eikonidia* have no the money value but they to have the spiritual worth to the good orthodox. I could to give them to the churchgoer who is the voter…"

"The voter?" I queried.

"The devote?" he suggested.

"I think you mean devotional."

"Yes, the devotional churchgoer would to treasure the icon."

I bit back a smile of amusement at Andreas' description of his flock. The Greeks that I often spotted sneaking out of the church for a crafty cigarette and a gossip struck me as the type more obligated to attend out of a sense of duty rather than religious fervour. Even his own mother admitted to sleeping through his sermons.

"Please, take the icons for your congregation. Consider it my donation to the church," I generously offered. Apart from giving the odd fifty cents for the votive candles at the Easter scrum, I must confess to being a bit miserly in my contributions to the local church.

"*Kathiste.*" Ordering us to sit down, Maria placed a piping hot platter of *loukoumades* on the table, light, fluffy and fried to perfection. A generous drizzle of local honey, a sprinkling of cinnamon and a handful of roughly chopped pistachios, completed the sweet masterpiece. Maria joined us, cackling as the hot doughnuts burnt her tongue. My glass was filled with the nasty cheap plonk from the plastic bottle of red that the Papas had purchased that morning. It tasted even viler than usual as the honeyed sweetness of the loukoumades exaggerated its vinegary tones. Conversation lapsed as the three of us tucked greedily into the honeyed dessert, savouring the sweetness. I considered that if I was up half the night glugging Gaviscon it would be a price well worth paying. Catching me surreptitiously loosening my belt, Maria gave me a knowing wink.

"*Pos einai i mitera sas? Pote erchetai stin Ellada?*" Chomping on a doughnut, Maria asked how my mother was and when she was coming to Greece.

I told her that Barry and Vangelis were hard at work transforming the *apothiki* into habitable quarters so that Violet Burke would have her own private space when she returned.

"*Tha meinai yia perissotero apo mia i dyo evdo-madades sti Meli?*" Maria asked if my mother would stay for more than a week or two in Meli. With my mouth full of *loukoumades*, I confirmed with a nod that mother would stay longer. Belatedly realising that Maria would likely interpret my nod as a no, I gulped down my doughnuts, telling Maria that I hoped that my mother would stay on for most of the winter: "*Elpizo oti i mitera tha meinei yia to megalytero meros tou cheimona.*"

As Maria beamed with pleasure at my response, my thoughts drifted back to my last encounter with Violet Burke. My visit to her new home had firmly cemented my belief that she would be better off ensconced in my downstairs storage.

Chapter 17

A Toy Boy or Two

My flying visit to Warrington to give Violet Burke a hand to move from her flat above the chippy to a ground floor council flat had more than cemented my determination that mother should spend a good chunk of the year with us. It was immediately apparent that the neighbourhood was patently unsuitable: one needn't step further than next door to trip over all manner of riff-raff. No sooner had the three of us pulled up outside Violet Burke's new dwelling in Benjamin's car than the low-life next door put in an unwelcome appearance.

"Here Vi, got yourself a couple of toy boys, I see. You always did like 'em young. You had a good ten years on, Arthur."

A vulgar wolf-whistle accompanied the words spat at my mother by a clearly uncouth harridan clad in a saggy pink velour tracksuit stretched out of shape. The catcalling neighbour propped up the adjacent doorway, arms solidly folded, thoroughly settled in for the duration in order to scrutinise our comings and goings and to give my mother's belongings the beady eyed once-over. Considering the woman bordered on the obese, I doubt that she had donned the exercise outfit with its intended purpose in mind.

About to defend my mother's honour by pointing out that I was her son, rather than her paramour, Vi warned me, "Just ignore her, don't give her the satisfaction." We silently made our way inside, struggling under the weight of a couple of cardboard boxes we had crammed in the boot, intensely aware of being under the microscope.

Exchanging questioning glances with Benjamin, I pondered the implication of Violet Burke refusing to put the neighbour straight by acknowledging me as her son. Such recognition would surely scupper what may well become malicious rumours that she had a toy boy or two in tow. Despite my mother often being a public embarrassment, I had made no effort to hide our relationship when she visited us in Greece: although initially reluctant, I had publicly admitted that she belonged to me. It struck me that perhaps my mother considered me an embarrassment. Once the outrageous notion was planted in my head, I had to voice it.

"Mother, are you ashamed of me? Surely you would prefer to acknowledge me as your son rather than have your neighbours maligning your name by saying that you have taken up with a toy boy."

"Don't be so daft, lad. What on earth made you think I'm ashamed of you? I'm that proud of you and Benjamin, I could fair burst," Violet Burke declared. "I just don't want the likes of Edna Billings knowing my business, that's all."

"Billings," I repeated. "You mean to say that yobbish woman outside who has poured her flab into that nasty tracksuit is the same Mrs Billings who came in the chippy for plaice every Friday."

"Aye, it is that. I told you that the council

had housed me next door to her."

"Yes, I remember now. I knew that you had no great liking for her but I hadn't imagined she would be nearly so rough," I said.

"She's rough, all right, and the gob on her is something else. She had a right go at me not that long ago in the chippy, dredging up Arthur even though he's been buried nigh on twenty years. Tempers flared, I can tell you. After a few choice words, she chucked her freshly fried plaice at me before I had chance to wrap it in newspaper. You just wouldn't credit how common some people can be. Course I had the last laugh, the stupid cow had already paid for it. She nearly turned violent when I refused to fry another one on the house," my mother revealed.

I was frankly appalled by my mother's tale of such plebeian behaviour; hurling fried plaice at a pensioner was beyond the pale. Benjamin, cringing beside me, clearly shared my sense of opprobrium. I couldn't help wondering if my son also shared my curiosity as to why Arthur Burke had been a bone of contention between the two women so long after he had been flattened by the number 47.

"Here Victor, sit down a minute. You too, Benjamin," mother invited. Since the man with the very small van that mother had hired to transport her few bits of furniture hadn't turned up yet, the invitation to sit proved a bit tricky. She finally directed us to perch on the boxes that we had carted in from the car.

"The pair of you might not like what I have to tell you, but I'll feel better for getting it off my chest. I just hope that you don't think the lesser of me when you've heard me out. I'd hate it if you disowned me."

Taking a seat, I braced myself for hearing something that could, by the sound of it, put a spoke in my new found relationship with my mother. Benjamin squeezed in next to me, leaving the other cardboard box free for Violet Burke to perch on. As she lowered her bulbous frame onto the box, I crossed my fingers that it would hold her weight; I didn't fancy having to haul her up from the floor if the cardboard collapsed. Violet Burke took a deep breath. Yanking a handkerchief out from her sleeve, she spat on it, using it to rub at an invisible speck on her dress.

"Apart from Dot at the chippy who is sworn to secrecy, no one knows that I've got a son or a grandson. The people round here have known me for years from the chippy, you see. I couldn't think of any way of telling them that my son had come back into my life without fessing up that I had abandoned you in the first place." Violet Burke stared at the floor as she spoke, wringing the life out of the handkerchief.

Finally raising her head, she looked me directly in the eye. "I'm not ashamed of you, Victor, I could never be that. I'm ashamed of what I did, of leaving you in that bucket and walking away as if it was nothing. All those years I lived with what I did, telling myself it was for the best. But when I finally found you and got to know you, got to know what a decent and good man you are, that's when it really hit me what a terrible thing I'd done."

"Oh, Mother," I sighed, leaning forward and taking her hand.

"Let me finish, Victor. You had the measure of that Billings woman, right enough; she's a spiteful piece of low-life and no mistake. I'd use more colourful language but I know how you wince when I let loose with the swear words."

"I think we could make allowances for any profanities in the circumstances," I assured her.

"Well, you can imagine how Edna Billings would look down her nose at me if the truth came out, if she knew that I'd abandoned my own son, my own flesh and blood. She'd have it blabbed all over the estate in two shakes of a dog's tail and she wouldn't miss a chance to rub my nose in it." Mother used the by now bedraggled handkerchief to dab at the solitary tear that threatened to turn into a flood.

"There's certainly no point in dragging up all that bucket business now. It's no one else's business," I concurred.

"Edna Billings would never let it drop if she got wind of it," mother said. "She'd just love to take the high road and let everyone know what a sorry excuse for a mother I've been. Her scum of a son might be doing a stretch for armed robbery, but at least she didn't walk away from him."

"She most likely dragged him up in awful circumstances which could well have been my fate too if you'd kept me, Mother. You mustn't punish yourself for giving me up. I have come to terms with it and long since forgiven you," I said. As the words left my mouth, I realised I had indeed pushed aside all traces of the lingering resentment which I had harboured for being abandoned in a bucket, even if I would never be able to come to terms with her terrible choice of receptacle. Even though six decades had passed, the indignity of being clad in a frilly pink bonnet and dumped in a coal bucket still made me cringe.

"You did what you had to do, Granny," Benjamin chimed in. "We don't think any less of you because of it."

"We understand that there was terrible stigma attached to having a baby out of wedlock," I added.

"And we know how difficult you had it back in the war, Granny, with no support from your family. Luckily you've got family around you now."

"That I have. I was that chuffed when the two of you came to help with the move. It's not as though either of you lives on the doorstep."

"And if my adoptive parents had still been alive when you finally crawled out of the woodwork, they would have personally thanked you for giving me up, Vi," I said. "They had resigned themselves to being childless until I came into their lives."

"They must have been that proud of you, Victor," my mother said.

"They were," I agreed, recalling their pride when I was accepted into the illustrious ranks of the Department of Food Standards and their excitement when I announced that Marigold had accepted my marriage proposal. "Since we attended Vic's funeral in Macclesfield, I have often shuddered at the thought that I may have turned out like my half-brother Terrance, if I hadn't had the advantages of the middle-class upbringing my adoptive parents were able to provide."

"He was another nasty piece of work, that Terrance. I have to say though it was uncanny how much he looked like you, Victor," Violet Burke said. "The spit he was. He looked more like you than his own father."

"It's strange to think that Dad has a double walking around," Benjamin laughed.

"I'd hardly go as far as that. I would call it more of a superficial resemblance," I argued, thankful that my son had been spared meeting his reprobate uncle.

"Aye, well Terrance has started to go to seed even though he is younger than you. That's what comes of being dragged up by the likes of Barb Foot," Violet Burke pronounced.

"Mother, you said that you got into a bit of a barney with that dreadful Billings woman about your fourth husband, Arthur Burke," I posited.

"Back in the day, me and Edna were what you'd call friendly acquaintances. She used to pop into the pub that I met Arthur in, made a right play for him she did. Even though her husband was inside, she liked to carry on as though she was single, throwing herself at anything with a pulse."

"I take it that you mean prison when you say inside. I'm getting confused, Granny, I thought you said that it was Edna Billing's son that is serving time."

"Like father, like son. I think Edna is the only Billings that hasn't been on the wrong side of a Strangeways bar. Anyway, as I was saying, Edna set her cap at Arthur, but he only had eyes for me..."

"But I thought that Arthur was a swindling bigamist..." I interrupted.

"Well he was, but that was more of a sideline for him, what he considered his line of work, not that I knew that until after he was dead. He'd never as much as flirt with another woman when he was with me. Anyway, Edna turned a right ugly shade of green when Arthur married me but it was nothing to the true colours she showed once it came out what he'd been up to. To this day she loves nowt more than having a dig and rubbing it in that I married a man that preyed on women."

"Whilst certainly not condoning what Arthur Burke did, surely it pales in comparison to armed robbery," I said, mentally referencing the crimes of the Billings menfolk.

"Well, I can't rightly say that those daft women who had their hearts broken and their savings accounts emptied would agree with you, Victor. Arthur left a trail of victims. I tried to do right by them by handing back any of their trinkets he'd lifted," Vi said, a look of weary exhaustion on her face. "It was a horrible business all round and I just wanted to put it behind me. Fat chance of that now that I'm forced to live next door to Edna Billings, she'll be dredging the whole sorry saga up every chance she gets and no mistake."

"It is quite unconscionable that you must endure the likes of such a ghastly woman living next door and making your life miserable," I stated angrily.

"It's a rum state of affairs but there's nowt I can do about it. The council won't budge...still you boys mustn't worry about me. I can give as good as I get."

"There *is* something you can do about it,

Mother. You can accept my offer to spend more time in Greece and move into the *apothiki*."

"That wife of yours won't want me under her feet all the time…"

"Once you are settled in the *apothiki* you won't be under her feet…well, only in the literal sense."

"Aye, let me think on it some more."

Chapter 18

Cuttlefish, Cod and Kippers

"V ictor, i mama sou..." Kyria Maria drummed her bony fingers impatiently on the table, reminding me that she had asked me about Violet Burke's intentions about staying on in Greece for more than the odd week or two.

Realising that I had been preoccupied with thoughts about my time back in Warrington, I gave myself a mental shake, replying, "*Elpizo i mitera mou na meinei yia merikous mines.*"

After saying that I hoped my mother would

stay on for a few months, I tried to explain that I wanted to get Violet Burke away from the less than salubrious neighbourhood she had recently moved to. Without wishing to tactlessly reveal any of my mother's secrets about her complicated past, I settled for a grammatically incorrect account of how ghastly the next door neighbour was. Struggling to come up with a Greek word descriptive enough to convey how frightful Mrs Billings really was, I rather feebly settled for "*Einai frikti,*" meaning she is horrible. Words failed me when I attempted to describe the sort of shiny nylon shell suits and the saggy track suits that were never designed with sport in mind that seemed to be all the rage with Violet Burke's new neighbours. Still, I imagine the visible flinch accompanying my words gave some indication of my feelings.

Try as I might, I could not keep up with the apparent vitriol that spewed from Maria's mouth when she launched into a lengthy diatribe only punctuated by dramatic gestures, her arms waving around like an out of control windmill. Spotting my frustration at being unable to decipher Maria's meaning, Andreas shushed his mother before offering a translation.

V.D. BUCKET

"*Mama* to know all about the bad neighbour because she to live next door to the pig for twenty year until he to fall off the roof. She say that was the happy day…"

Andreas paused in his translation to switch to Greek, shouting at his mother that she couldn't go around expecting him to repeat that she was happy that Pedros had met his maker. Indeed, such sentiments were most inappropriate when uttered from the mouth of a cleric.

"*Alla einai alitheia,*" Maria shrugged, her bottom lip jutting out in righteous indignation. I didn't need Andreas to translate she had said, 'But it is true.'

"*Xechnas oti einai papas. Den prepei na milao yia tous nekrous,*" Andreas retorted, stating that she forgets he is a Papas and he must not speak ill of the dead.

As mother and son sniped at one another, apparently forgetting they had a guest, I recalled that Maria and the previous owner of my home had been on bad terms for over two decades. Following a particularly vitriolic tiff over the public bins, Maria had resorted to burning her rubbish in the back garden rather than risk having Pedros poke through her personal waste. The resultant noxious smoke drove her despised neighbour ballistic, an unexpected benefit in Maria's eyes since she derived enormous enjoyment from tormenting him. Unfortunately, her disgusting habit of burning plastic did not end with his death; the practice had become so ingrained that we regularly choked on the filthy fumes from Maria's bonfires when we first took up residence.

I was rather taken aback to say the least when Maria continued, "*Makari na borousa na apallago apo ton geitona pou zei ekei tora.*" To hear her say that she wished she could get rid of the neighbour who lives there now, cut me to the quick. I was definitely under the impression that we muddled along quite nicely, an opinion surely confirmed by my stomach full of dumplings. It was only when Maria added, "*Fanatei frikto sto esoroucho tou,*" meaning 'he looks horrible in his underpants' that it dawned on me that the neighbour she wished to be rid of was Guzim, rather than me. Perish the thought that I would ever flaunt myself in front of my elderly neighbour clad in nothing but my underpants: I would never dream of making such an undignified spectacle of myself.

"*To ntous tou Guzim einai krymmeno piso apo mia kourtina tora,*" I said. Maria's face broke into a wrinkled smile of relief when I told her that Guzim's shower was now hidden behind a curtain.

"*Sta alethia*?" Maria demanded to know if it was true.

"*Sigoura*." 'Certainly,' I reassured her

It did not escape my notice that Papas Andreas' face fell upon hearing this exchange. Perhaps he had quite fancied spying on Luljeta if she was in the habit of hosing herself off in the mornings. He had certainly appeared more enthusiastic when I had mistakenly offered him a young woman than he had over the bag of worthless old icons.

I told Maria that when I left my mother's new flat in Warrington she had given me a bulging suitcase stuffed with winter apparel to bring back with me on the plane to Greece, to save her the bother of lugging it over herself. Apart from almost passing out from shock when I was fleeced for some exorbitant sum for the excess weight at the airport, the suitcase had reassured me more than any words could that Violet Burke intended to make her next stay in Meli a long one.

"*Victor, tha me pas ti Violet yia me na agoraso xana to psari*?" Maria rubbed her gnarled fingers together gleefully as she asked if I would take her and Violet to buy fish again.

"*Isos*." I hoped that my subdued reply of 'perhaps' was suitably non-committal. I had no desire to suffer a repetition of our last visit to the coastal village where the local fisherman sold their catch from a marble slab at the harbour first thing in the mornings.

When mother had last stayed with us here during the summer, she had arrived armed with photographs of fish to use as a language ice-breaker with Maria. Violet Burke's attempts to school Maria in the English words for plaice, haddock and cod hit a bit of a road block because it was impossible to identify a single fish beneath their breaded and battered coatings. I must take full responsibility for the outing that followed since it had been me that put the idea in Violet Burke's head that they may make more linguistic progress if they used actual fish for reference rather than photos of deep fried ones.

After confirming that dead fish would no doubt do nicely for their purpose, I was roped into taking the two old women down to the coast at the crack of dawn on my next free morning. In spite of my best efforts, I was unable to wriggle out of the commitment once made; I couldn't persuade Marigold to join us at such an unspeakable hour even though her presence would have potentially watered down the company. The thought of being stuck translating between Violet Burke and Kyria Maria was one that filled me with mind-numbing boredom. Their conversation was banal at the best of times yet both parties remained ignorant of this fact due to their total inability to communicate with each other. Perhaps they imagined that if only they could decipher each other's words, they would be in for a treat of scintillating dialogue.

The two elderly women talked at each other non-stop on the drive to the coast, their witless chatter peppered with demands to know what the other was saying in two languages. I began to lose the will to live as my ears were subjected to a constant barrage of, "What's she saying now?" from my mother and an endless volley of the same question in Greek, *"Ti leei?"* from Kyria Maria. In order to demonstrate the lengths I was prepared to suffer to facilitate their growing friendship, I will pen an example of their jabbering as we made our way through the village and down to the coast. For the sake of my sanity I will write Maria's Greek words in English.

As I overtook Panos' tractor, Maria sniped, "Panos is up and about early. Pity he didn't have time for a wash."

"What's she saying?" Violet Burke demanded.

"She said that Panos is about early this morning, no doubt he has a heavy workload ahead in the fields."

"He grows a good potato, I'll give him that. They make excellent chips," mother conceded.

"What's she saying?" Maria demanded to know.

"Mother fancies some chips for breakfast," I duly informed Maria.

"A proper Greek breakfast is yoghurt with honey," Maria declared.

"What's she saying," my mother snapped.

"Maria says that Greek yoghurt will put some hairs on your chest," I translated, making it up as I drove along.

You get the drift and it didn't improve. I took a vow of silence when Violet Burke expected me to describe what I believe may well be the uniquely British habit of eating kippers for breakfast. I really don't envisage it ever catching on with the Greeks.

By the time I parked up in the small fishing

V.D. BUCKET

village, it was already bustling with swarthy fishermen bringing their boats back to harbour and unloading their catch of the day from their nets and lines. As they worked, they hollered across to one another, comparing their catches, those with the biggest hauls mocking the fishing prowess of those with nothing more to their name than a bucket of tiddlers. My two companions were happy with my suggestion that we relax with a coffee at the *kafenion* overlooking the harbour before we got down to the brass tacks of attempting to identify fish that weren't disguised by a deep fried covering.

Sitting side by side, Kyria Maria and Violet Burke presented a strange pairing, Maria bone-thin and clad in her usual black widow's weeds, Violet Burke bulbous and overdone in something straining at the seams. I would hazard a guess that it was fashioned out of something resembling tweed but I don't claim to be an expert on women's clothing. Maria's makeup free wrinkled face sprouted a stubborn black hair on her chin that I itched to pluck. The rectangular glasses perched on the end of Violet Burke's nose magnified the thick layer of blue eye shadow that she had slapped on haphazardly, presumably without the aid of a mirror:

perchance she had mistaken our early morning fish jaunt for a night down the pub. Whereas Maria had let nature take its course, her wispy hair now white, Violet Burke's locks were brazenly red, the product of a recent home colour job with a bottle of cheap dye. I imagined that to the casual observer it would look as though a sweet old granny, the butter wouldn't melt type, was out and about with her sometime slapper friend who refused to grow old gracefully. I chortled to myself, thinking how deceptive looks could be. Anyone in the know would realise that I was saddled with a pair of bossy old harridans.

"What's so funny, Victor?" my mother demanded.

"Nothing. I was just recalling taking coffee at this very same table with Panos when we drove Guzim to the clinic for his tetanus shot after Panos' guard dog took a chunk out of his buttock. I'd never realised that dogs were partial to sardines until then."

"I wish I'd been there to see that Guzim having a chunk taken out of him," mother chuckled.

"It wasn't funny at the time," I assured her, shooing away a stray cat that had popped up at the mention of sardines.

The adjacent tables soon filled up with local fishermen ordering coffee and casting bemused glances in our direction. No doubt the sight of an elderly Greek lady sipping coffee with an English gent rather threw them for a loop. Goodness only knew what they made of Violet Burke being thrown in the mix. Fortunately, Thomas, the local fisherman who drives his catch up to Meli to sell, recognised me. In no time at all he was explaining to his cronies that I am somewhat of a local. Kyria Maria was of course well known in these parts. Although she rarely gets out of Meli these days, her reputation preceded her. As the mother of a very popular Papas, she was afforded a modicum more of respect than she likely deserved.

"I can't fathom how anyone can stomach this Greek coffee, it's nowt but froth and grinds," Violet Burke complained, staring at the tiny cup in disdain. Downing her coffee in one, she grimaced at the strong taste, revealing the thick coating of ground dregs stuck to her teeth.

"Would you like me to order you a nice cup of tea instead, Mother?"

"Don't bother; it'll likely be swimming with twigs. I think we should go and check out the fish before all these stray cats start giving them a licking. Happen they'll have some nice kippers we can take home for breakfast. They'll be a real treat for Maria."

I blanched, sincerely hoping that no kippers had managed to swim into Greek waters to infiltrate the daily catch. I could only imagine Marigold's reaction if she rolled out of bed to discover Kyria Maria tucking into a breakfast of kippers in our kitchen. I would never hear the end of it. I rather suppose that kippers are on the banned list along with bacon, Marigold tending to ban any foods that create a lingering smell.

The fish market was simplicity itself, comprising nothing more than a marble slab affixed to the harbour wall and a set of old-fashioned cumbersome weighing scales. The fisherman displayed their choicest fish on the slab, having already put aside the fish that were destined for taverna kitchens and local households. The fishermen gathered round the slab, smoking and chatting, exchanging the odd fish for coinage as the local women made their purchases. There was no need for the hard sell: the locals could spot a good fish when they saw it.

My fingers went into overdrive, flicking through my trusty Greek to English dictionary in a desperate effort to keep pace with the names of the fish that Kyria Maria rattled off. I must confess that my knowledge of foreign fish was pretty basic at that point and I was unable to distinguish a *barbourni* from a *kefalos*, though the dictionary enlightened me that they were both types of mullet, the *barbourni* being the red variety and the *kefalos* a grey flathead. The translation of *kefalos* reminded me of the way that the elderly lady I had run into in the clinic insisted that Albanians bore the distinguishing feature of flat heads, a theory I had dismissed as nothing more than stuff and nonsense.

Fortunately, Ilias, a taverna owner from one of the neighbouring villages, put in an appearance, a stroke of luck since he spoke excellent English and was extremely knowledgeable about all the different types of fish on display. As we had eaten in his establishment a number of times, he greeted me like a long lost friend, happy to assume the role of translator between my two cantankerous companions. It soon became apparent that poor Ilias had landed himself with a thankless task indeed considering the sneering reaction Violet Burke had upon being informed that *soupia* was a cuttlefish.

"Call that sorry looking thing a fish, it's just plain nasty. I always say you can't trust anything with whiffy tentacles. And just look at its mouth, it's unnatural. It looks like it's about to chew down on its own intestines with those teeth. You'd never catch me frying one of those up in the chippy."

I bit my tongue; it seemed unnecessarily callous to remind my mother that her chippy days would soon be behind her. Plus she was getting a bit long in the tooth to be persuaded that tentacles could really be very tasty. Whilst I do enjoy a nicely done squid or octopus tentacle when dining out, I had yet to be brave enough to experiment with preparing them in my own kitchen.

"Not to fry the *soupia*, it is the delectable with the *spanaki*, the spinach…" Ilias protested, fixing his deep brown eyes on my mother and smiling in a measured way that revealed his dimples.

"I'm not sold on greens to be honest…" Violet Burke said, her tone becoming less obstreperous as Ilias worked his charm.

"Well, you're inordinately fond of mushy peas and they're green," I interrupted.

"That's a cod," Violet Burke shouted, grabbing Maria's arm and repeating, "Cod, cod," emphatically as she pointed at a silvery fish.

"No, it is what we call the *lavraki*, I think in English the sea bass," Ilias corrected.

"Cod and chips." Kyria Maria said, her face transformed by an enormous grin as she sounded out the new words, convinced that she had mastered a bit of English.

"That's it Maria, you've got it. Cod is the English word for *lavraki*," Violet Burke blustered, puffed up with her own importance. Ilias caught my eye and winked, not bothering to explain to them that *bakalaos* was actually the Greek word for cod. He caught on fast.

The words cod and chips, and *lavraki me patates*, reverberated in my ears on the drive home, both women clutching a carrier bag containing the catch of the day that most appealed. To my immense relief the pair of them made a dash for Maria's kitchen on our return, Maria desperate to prove to my mother that cuttlefish was edible, Violet Burke eager to give a practical demonstration of how to make cod and chips out of a sea bass. On reflection it would have been easier to simply send the pair of them to Tina's to buy some of the dried *bakalaos* that are sold from enormous wooden tubs packed with salt.

"Victor, akous." Maria demanding to know if I was listening to her snapped me out of my reverie.

"Of course," I lied before remembering to switch to Greek. *"Fysika."*

"Eipa oti itan toso kali mera me Violet. I mitera sou einai exairetiki perea," Maria said she had reminded me that was a good day out with Violet and that my mother was excellent company.

Realising that it would be prudent to make a hasty escape before Maria attempted to pin me down to a return visit to the fish slab, I surreptitiously buckled my belt. Telling them that I needed to be getting home as I had an early start on Pegasus, Andreas thanked me again for the worthless icons whilst Maria busied herself spooning *loukoumades* into a plastic tub. Pressing said tub into my hands, she told me to take it home for my wife.

"Oti i gynaika sou chreizetai na taisei, einai poly lepti sto miso."

I suppressed a snort of amusement as Maria told me that my wife needed feeding up, voicing the opinion that Marigold is too thin by half. It struck me as ludicrous that my stick-thin elderly neighbour should pass such judgement on Marigold who has maintained her perfect figure.

Still, I made a mental note to repeat Maria's words to Marigold if she was still awake when I arrived home: my wife would be sure to interpret the critical words as a compliment.

Chapter 19

A Clandestine Meeting

I t was barely light when I awoke the next morning, thankful that my final trip on Pegasus for the year offered a means of escaping our irritating houseguests for the day. The heartburn I had anticipated whilst wolfing down Maria's *loukoumades* had mercifully been kept at bay with a hearty swig of Gaviscon before retiring. I felt a slight twinge of sorrow that this would be my last excursion with *Kapetanios* Vasos until the next tourist season rolled round again: after all, a life on the ocean wave has a certain appeal in small doses. Aware that my seafaring legs would be relegated to dry land until next summer, I was greatly relieved that Tina's offer of managing the shop spared me from being slung on the scrapheap of the unemployed for the foreseeable.

Raring to go, I headed to the shower, only to discover the bathroom was occupied. Pressing my ear against the door, I could just make out the sound of the running shower. Since Marigold was still hogging the lightweight summer duvet, I surmised that either Geraldine or Ashley was up and about already. It really was the most dreadful nuisance to have the smooth running of my morning routine interfered with, particularly on a working day. Moreover, the intolerable prospect of being forced to make small talk over coffee loomed. Considering there is nothing more galling than having the peace and quiet of my first coffee of the day disturbed by inane chatter, I was tempted to wake Marigold and demand that she play the good hostess. Since that would simply mean an extra body disturbing my peace, I resisted the urge to ruin my wife's lie in.

Waiting for the coffee to brew, I occupied my time by opening a couple of tins of cat food for Catastrophe and Clawsome, and treated Pickles to a tin of sardines as a reward for his well-timed performance the previous evening. I began to feel increasingly on edge. Whoever was hogging the bathroom was in danger of making me late; I needed to shower and dress. Turning up at Pegasus unwashed and still in my pyjamas would not do at all: even though it would barely raise an eyebrow from the pungent *Kapetanios* who is all too accustomed to throwing grubby clothes on over his sweaty body, it would almost certainly guarantee a slew of negative comments on the customer satisfaction surveys.

Striding out on the balcony, I took my first sip of strong coffee, the welcome brew going some way to ease my annoyance. The sheer joy of stepping outdoors and drinking in the wonderful view of the sea on the horizon as it becomes discernible in first light is something I cherish on a daily basis. Thinking I would soon be ahoy on the clear blue sea brought a smile to my face. Since it was the last trip of the season, I pondered throwing caution to the wind and perhaps taking a dip from the boat on the way back to land in the afternoon. Cynthia would be sure to turn a blind eye to her brother-in-law bending the rules: she rarely went out of her way to be a jobsworth.

Taking a hearty breath of the crisp clean air, rich with the tangy scent of lemon blossom, gave me an appreciation for life that I had never experienced to the same degree back in Manchester. The prospect of the long drive up to town was not unpleasant when compared to being stuck in a traffic jam on the Manchester ring road. Certainly the views are incomparable. I much prefer to be held up by a herd of goats on the road rather than be stuck behind an interminably slow moving line of assorted vehicles belching exhaust fumes in my face.

My ruminations were disturbed by Ashley putting in an appearance in the kitchen. Since he was dressed, I surmised that it must have been him rather than Geraldine that had been wallowing so inconsiderately in the shower all this time. I noticed that Ashley's great height seemed somewhat reduced this morning but the incongruity in his size was explained by the dreadful way he was slouching. I doubt that the sofa bed in my office had offered the most comfortable night since it was rather on the short side. Still, he had only himself to blame, the discomfort could have been avoided if he had simply bunked in with his girlfriend.

"Good Morning," I called over from the balcony. Ashley, clearly unaware that I was lurking in the shadows, unfolded himself, the slouch disappearing as he stretched to his full height.

"There's coffee on the table, do help yourself," I offered, reluctantly joining him in the kitchen. "Afraid I can't stop to chat, I need to grab a shower before I leave for work."

"I was under the impression that you were retired."

"Only in England. Here in Greece, I am gainfully employed," I assured him, attempting not to gawp too obviously at the bizarre transformation of his hair, revealed in all its glory at close quarters. My morning instantly brightened, my mood positively lifted.

Whereas only the day before, Ashley's hair had been precisely contoured around his large protruding ears, now the same ears were concealed with hair combed over them and a few straggly bits to spare. Not only had his hair apparently grown several inches overnight, it had also changed colour, morphing from dark to mousy brown. I immediately discounted the theory that a couple of days under the Greek sunshine had lightened his hair, instead plumping for the obvious answer that Ashley was sporting a wig. Such a theory would of course explain the tinge of nylon that his glossy bouffant locks had displayed at our first meeting. Deciding it would be impolite to comment, I struggled to contain my laughter until I could safely lock the bathroom door behind me. Turning on the shower, I wondered if Geraldine was aware that her new fellow's hair wasn't the real deal. He didn't strike me as the type of chap to encourage his girlfriend to run her fingers through it.

Despite his ridiculous new barnet, it was Ashley who managed the last laugh, having run off every last drop of hot water. Being forced to shower under an icy jet rather killed my good mood, as did Ashley's snort of derision when I reappeared in the kitchen kitted out in my repping uniform, the flame resistant modacrylic polo shirt emblazoned with a large Greek flag. Apart from being forced to display a whistle on a string around my neck, I saw nothing to particularly amuse in my current uniform: I was certainly thankful that Ashley hadn't clocked me in the previous orange Tango design. Now that had made me look like a real plonker.

"I'm afraid that you'll have to entertain

yourself until the ladies get up since I need to be on my way. Do feel free to enjoy a stroll around the garden and make the acquaintance of the chickens," I said. Recalling that Luljeta may be making her own intimate acquaintance with Guzim's outdoor hosepipe, I hastily added, "Please don't wander through the hole in the fence, it leads to private land belonging to my Albanian neighbour."

Admittedly land was rather overstating the postage stamp size plot that Guzim's shed stood on, but it struck me as unfair to leave the Albanian shed dweller to the mercy of Ashley bumbling through the gap in the wooden fence if his curiosity got the better of him.

"I may well delay exploring the garden until Geraldine gets up. That's if she ever gets up of course, I've noticed she has the unfortunate tendency of being quite lazy," Ashley responded. I raised my eyebrows without responding, recalling that the last time she'd visited Geraldine had sprang out of bed at the crack of dawn to attend to her spiritual needs at the church. "Yes, I'll leave the garden until Geraldine surfaces."

"Ah quite, nothing like appreciating the beauty of the great outdoors together," I said.

"I was thinking it might offer an escape. You probably noticed that Geraldine's attentions can be a bit cloying."

Something in Ashley's superior tone rubbed me the wrong way. With one foot out of the door, I hesitated, reflecting that Marigold would be most put out to hear her good friend spoken of in such a disparaging way. Although not one to generally defend Geraldine, I felt it was my duty to speak up on her behalf.

"Perhaps it's none of my business and not my place to say anything about your relationship with Geraldine..."

"You're right, it really isn't..." Ashley interrupted.

"Well, I fully intend to speak my piece anyway," I said, my firm tone brooking no argument. "Due to her friendship with Marigold, I have known Geraldine for quite a long time. She's not a bad old stick really and certainly deserves better than you. The way you spoke down to her yesterday evening was shabby to say the least. If you don't reciprocate her feelings perhaps you should call it a day instead of dragging things out. Do let her down gently though, she can be prone to histrionics."

The way in which Ashley's mouth flapped

open and closed in shock made him resemble a dying fish gasping for air.

Having said my piece, I fired a parting shot before leaving, repeating the stock line that Marigold had trotted out on at least a dozen occasions. "All Geraldine wants is to find someone to settle down with. She deserves to be happily married."

Since Geraldine was still on my mind as I started up the Punto, I thought my eyes were deceiving me when after driving to the village square to turn the car around, I spotted the back of a familiar woman hovering outside the church. Naturally my initial thought was that it must be a coincidence since Geraldine was surely still tucked up in bed.

Wary of backing into Spiros' hearse as I negotiated a three-point turn with one eye fixed on the woman, the Punto stalled in spectacular fashion when I saw a bearded black clad figure appear in the church vestibule, his outstretched arm drawing the woman inside. It looked like the celibate cleric and my houseguest were up to their old tricks of clandestine meetings in church.

Chapter 20

Along for the Ride

Much as I was tempted to floor the accelerator and zoom right by, my innate good manners obliged me to stop when I spotted Milton lurking at the new bus stop. Pulling up alongside him, I enquired what he was doing out and about at such an early hour. It struck me as highly doubtful that he was waiting for an actual bus because the only one of the day wasn't due to arrive for another hour.

"Ah, Victor, I am waiting for the bus up to

town, old chap."

"I think you'll find it doesn't come along for another hour," I enlightened him.

"One can never be too careful. I heard that the Greek woman, Kyria Kom, Kompo, Kompouloulou…the one with the long unpronounceable name that sounds like compost…

"Kyria Kompogiannopoulou," I suggested, thinking that even the Greek translation of compost, *koprochoma*, sounded nothing remotely like her name.

"That's the one, can't get my tongue around it at all. Anyway, I heard that she missed her hospital appointment last week because the bus came along ten minutes early. Shocking the way these Greeks can't stick to a timetable, just shocking. I thought things would have improved since they had all that practice organising the Olympic Games this summer."

"They operate on Greek time. I'm heading up to town myself if you fancy a lift," I heard myself offering. Although reluctant to proffer an invitation which meant I would be obligated to make small talk for the duration, it was undoubtedly the decent thing to do. After all, Milton had thrown himself into the bins to retrieve Marigold's curtains without a second thought for his dodgy artificial hip.

"Very decent of you, old chap," Milton replied, hurling himself into the passenger seat with gay abandon before I could have second thoughts. For a pensioner with a shaky hip he was remarkably nimble.

"So, what takes you to town today?" I asked.

"Cat food, old chap, cat food. Edna threw a bit of a wobbler when she caught me feeding the adopted ferals with that luxury brand I retrieved from the bins. She sounded like one of those blasted health inspectors the way she went on about it being unhygienic."

Biting my tongue as Milton disparaged my illustrious former profession, I muttered, "Surely she can appreciate that with your penurious finances free cat food is all that you can afford. You really shouldn't encourage her to take in every waif and stray that she trips over."

"Can't be done, old chap. Edna has a heart of gold, can't see a cat without giving it a home. Anyway, she refused to see reason when I pointed out that the food from the bins was cheaper than the tins from the village shop. She said if I was that desperate to save money on cat food, I must take myself up to Lidl and stock up on bargain brands."

"Is she aware that the bus route doesn't actually go anywhere near Lidl which is on the outskirts of town? You'll have a long walk across town with your dodgy hip."

"Can't say I gave any thought to an actual bus route. I rather thought that one just announced one's destination to the driver on boarding."

"Buses don't tend to operate on quite the same line as taxis," I told him, somewhat shocked by his naiveté. "Have you ever actually used public transport?"

"Can't say that I have, old chap, not unless one counts that frightfully dusty journey from Nairobi to Marangu when the old Land Rover was relieved of its tyres; couldn't get far on just treads, what oh. It was no fun doing nearly 200 miles on a rickety bus squashed up against a voluptuous native holding a squirming chicken, I can tell you," Milton guffawed. "The way she was squeezing my thigh, I fully expected her clan to announce that I'd have to make an honest woman out of her when we arrived. I must confess, I broke out in a terrible sweat trying to work out the Swahili for 'I'm already spoken for.' I couldn't see Edna being too amused if I was forced to bring home a second wife, even though it was legal out there."

"Quite, one wife is more than enough for any man," I agreed. "Still, it's doubtful that you will need to contend with such scenarios on the local bus. Have you arranged transport home for when you've finished your shopping?"

"I intend to get the bus back, old chap," Milton said, apparently oblivious that the return bus didn't operate until late afternoon.

"You'll have an awfully long wait," I said, informing him of the rather limited timetable.

"Drat and blast, I had no idea. Rather thought I'd just be able to hail a bus home when I'd finished at Lidl. I must say you seem awfully well informed for a chap with a vehicle at your disposal."

"Well, there's been a lot of talk about the new bus service in the village and how the timetable isn't exactly what one would describe as convenient…"

"Ah yes, makes sense you being in the know, being able to speak the same lingo as the natives and all that."

Bristling at Milton's casual dismissal of the locals as natives and his stubborn refusal to learn any Greek, I resigned myself to either abandoning him in town for the day or being stuck with him. The stark reality was that Milton most likely had empty pockets with nothing beyond the wherewithal to pay for a few tins of cat food. I doubted he had the means to keep himself entertained until late afternoon, particularly as most of the town closed down for the afternoon siesta. Call me an old softie, but I must confess that I didn't like the thought of him wandering round at a loose end on his dodgy hip.

"I promised Marigold that I would pick up some shopping at Lidl on my way home," I said, recalling that my wife had told me to buy a case of cheap red as she found the plastic stuff embarrassing in front of her guests. "I suppose the best thing all round would be for you to join me on Pegasus for the day and then we can stop in at Lidl for your cat food when we disembark."

"Wouldn't dream of being a burden, old chap…"

"Really, it's no trouble," I said, attempting to convince myself that it really wasn't. "We'll find you a quiet spot to while away the day on deck. Of course I won't be able to wangle you a ticket for the main attraction but I'll be able to sneak you a free lunch at the Captain's table."

"Oh I say, Edna will be impressed. She's always fancied hobnobbing at a Captain's table with all the dignitaries."

"I think you've got rather the wrong end of the stick. The Captain's table is simply the table in the taverna where the crew eat…"

"The crew?"

"*Kapetanios* Vasos and his mute sidekick Sami. And me, of course, though technically I'm not crew. Perhaps you met Vasos at Barry's wedding; he made quite the impression in pink velvet…"

"Can't say I did, old chap. Rather avoided that whole shebang on account of not wanting Edna to run into Violet Burke. By the way how is your dear mother getting on? Such a splendid woman."

Sighing inwardly, I wondered if I had completely lost my marbles by inviting Milton to tag along. Since I had no intention of discussing my mother with him, I adroitly changed the subject.

"I rather fancy that I inherited my skill in the kitchen from my mother, although our tastes tend to differ quite drastically. She's more into chips and lard whilst I favour fresh local ingredients and olive oil. I've had the germ of an idea of conducting cookery classes over the winter…not a word to Marigold though, it's still early days," I warned.

"You can count on me to keep schtum, old chap. Have to say it's a spiffing idea, what. I'd do it myself if I could cook but I can't seem to find my way round the dratted kitchen. Bit of a disaster all round on the domestic front."

"Indeed, there seems to be a dearth of expertise on the culinary front amongst the local expats. That's actually what inspired my idea of cooking lessons…"

"You'd be a natural, old chap. That garlicky thing that you cooked up for the last expat dinner party was just the ticket…never thought that cold soup could actually be edible but you proved me wrong."

"Ah yes, that was a Spanish dish, Sopa de Ajo. Of course, I intend to only teach Greek dishes in my classes…"

"I say, perhaps I should sign up for lessons. Imagine Edna's face if I managed to cook something edible for supper."

"Well, as I said, it's early days yet, nothing concrete," I blustered. I really didn't want the likes of Milton cluttering up my kitchen. If I went ahead with my classes it would be with the express purpose of extracting a bob or two from rich expats like Sherry and Norman who had more money than sense. I had no intention of saddling myself with any charity cases when I had a living to earn.

Pulling into the small village that marked the half-way point to town, I decided to park up and call in the bakery for a takeout coffee and a bite to eat since I had left the house without any breakfast. Presuming that Milton had declined my offer of coffee due to being a bit strapped, I ordered two coffees anyway. The delicious aroma of freshly baked bread and pies was quite irresistible to my rumbling stomach as I perused the tempting array of snacks on offer, selecting two savoury pies to take back to the car.

"*Spanakopita* or *kotopita*," I said to Milton, giving him first dibs.

"I'm not with you, old chap," he replied.

"Do you prefer *spanakopita* or *kotopita*? I got one of each. My treat."

"I'm still not with you, old chap. Speak English, there's a good fellow."

"Would you like the spinach pie or the chicken one?" I translated, unable to credit that he wasn't familiar with the Greek names of such popular pies.

"Awfully good of you, I'll take the spinach

one," he declared, immediately devouring an enormous bite of the filo pastry stuffed with spinach and feta. Taking a gulp of coffee, he added, "No time for brekkie with having to leave so early. I say, this coffee is awfully good, first rate."

Recalling Edna's propensity to split one tea-spoonful of instant between three cups, I was happy to see Milton enjoying a strong shot of caffeine. As we set off again, Milton questioned why I wasn't eating.

"Not enough hands, I'm probably already flouting some obscure Greek traffic law by drinking my coffee on the go. I shall save my pie until we get to Pegasus," I replied. Judging by the mess of pastry crumbs littering my uphol-stery, I wished that Milton had managed to re-frain from tucking into his in the Punto. Still, I thought, with a bit of luck, Milton's preoccupa-tion with his breakfast would give me a break from his witless chatter.

As the Punto sped over the crest of the mountainous road, I was indeed granted a few minutes of peace and quiet, Milton apparently as captivated with the spectacular views as he was by his *spanakopita*. Shifting into the twists and turns of the winding road as it led down to town, we were afforded wonderful views, the expanse of the buzzing metropolis spread out on the horizon.

"It's certainly something to see," Milton remarked. "I don't get up here often enough with not having a vehicle. Still, things could change if the foreign rights are sold."

"The foreign rights?"

"To my book, old chap. There's mutterings about the Japanese wanting a translation."

"Really," I said in surprise. "Are they big on porn in Japan?"

"Erotica, old chap, erotica. It seems that the Japs have expressed an interest, along with the Frenchies."

"Well, I suppose with the French it's understandable. They do tend to have a reputation for being very permissive."

"If anything comes of it, I would appreciate your advice on picking out an old banger..."

"I think Barry's more your man for that," I suggested, belatedly realising that I may well have landed my brother-in-law in it. As Milton rambled on about what he could do with his new found riches if anything ever came of his book hitting the big time, I wished that Scarlet Bottom would put a sock in it. Since that seemed impossible, I simply tuned out. Remembering that this would be my last trip to town for work for the foreseeable, I wanted to bask in an appreciation of the panoramic vista.

Chapter 21

Scintillating Conversation

I say, old chap, exceedingly good looking ship," Milton commented as we walked the gangplank to Pegasus.

"It's a pleasure boat, not a Mr Kipling cake," I pointed out, steadying my elderly companion as he faltered on his dodgy hip. As much as his presence was an irritant I could do without, I didn't want to see him taking a spur-of-the-moment unwanted dip.

"Just wait here whilst I round up the Captain.

I need to clear it with him that you'll be on-board for the day."

"Quite, wouldn't do to be accused of being a stowaway and tossed overboard," Milton quipped.

"It shouldn't be a problem," I assured him. "Vasos is very much of the mind-set 'my home is your home.'"

"Ah, didn't realise he lived on the thing."

"He doesn't…"

"You just said it was his home."

"He does bed down here on occasion if he's too sozzled to make his way home," I clarified having forgotten how literally Milton took every word.

I was immensely relieved to discover no sign of *Kapetanios* Vasos in the wheel cabin as it meant that he had already crawled out of his pit, thus saving me the bother of acting as his personal alarm clock. Since there was no sign of him, I bellowed, "Vaso," hoping to alert him to my arrival.

"*Ela Victor, ti kaneis?*" Recognising the booming voice of Vasos, I looked around, still unable to locate him.

"*Pou eisai?*" I shouted back, asking him where he was.

"Edo kato." Upon hearing Vasos call out 'down here' I finally spotted him treading water in the sea. After swimming towards the ladder, Vasos hauled himself up the rungs, thoroughly soaking me as he greeted me with an enthusiastic bear hug, telling me, *"I thalassa einai kali yia to banio simera."*

I wasn't quite certain if he had just announced that the sea was good for swimming today or for taking a bath in; his words could be translated either way. Noticing the soap-on-a-rope slung around his neck and bouncing up and down on his hairy wet chest, I suspected the latter. I was glad to see that Vasos was making good use of the gift that Violet Burke had brought him from England; I have yet to come across a soap-on-a-rope in a Greek shop. Delighted that Vasos had purged himself of his usual persistent sweaty aroma, I sighed in exasperation when he grabbed a grubby old towel stinking of rancid perspiration, using it for a full body rub-down.

Introducing Milton, I told Vasos that I'd said it would be okay if he tagged along on our jaunt. *"Vaso, afto einai o filous mou Milton, eipa oti tha itan entaxei an irthe."*

Milton looked rather taken aback when Vasos

gripped his hand, greeting him by shouting, "Hello, Fray Bentos beautiful." I inwardly cursed Violet Burke for introducing these two new words to Vasos' limited English vocabulary. Although he was clueless to their meaning, he clearly liked the way they rolled off his tongue.

"Delighted to make your acquaintance, old chap," Milton yelled back.

"Vasos doesn't speak a word of English," I told Milton.

"Oh, rightio," Milton responded with a confused look on his face, obviously unfamiliar with Vasos' predilection for spewing random English words without any context. Upping his volume considerably, Milton repeated his words with painfully slow precision. "I said, delighted to make your acquaintance."

I might have guessed that Milton was the sort of Brit that held firm to the opinion that foreigners would soon get the gist of the conversation if only one spoke very slowly and loudly.

"*Ti?*" Vasos spluttered the Greek word for what.

"No thanks, old chap, but awfully kind of you to offer. I had a coffee in the car."

"Fray Bentos," Vasos replied, a broad beam

on his face.

"I couldn't possibly manage one on top of that spinach pie I had earlier," Milton replied.

"*Ti?*"

"Well I suppose if you insist on twisting my arm, milk and one sugar, thanks awfully."

"Sami." Spotting his mute sidekick slopping his mop around the upper deck, Vasos took the opportunity to escape.

"Darn nice fellow," Milton observed. "Seems you were mistaken when you said he doesn't speak English."

"He throws out the odd word. Don't take it the wrong way if he declares that he loves you at some point during the day," I said, not bothering to elaborate further. Milton's obtuseness led me to believe that he had never actually mastered any Swahili during his time in Africa but simply blustered his way through the continent, speaking at full volume whenever he encountered any locals.

"Now, if you just take a seat while I run through the numbers for today. Ah, not too many too cope with, just 30 signed up for the trip. They tend to drop off towards the end of the season."

Leaning over the railings, I furtively tucked

into the *kotopita* I'd purchased earlier, fully aware that I was flouting the company policy prohibiting eating food on-board. Since Vasos has extremely lax hygiene standards to say the least, I sometimes take the odd risk now that Tiffany is no longer around to enforce the rules. Sami could always mop up the odd crumb that I left in my wake.

I had just polished off the *kotopita*, a particular tasty treat filled with red peppers and feta in addition to chicken, when the first of the day's tourists began to wander towards the boat. Tripping across the gangplank, I took my place on the quayside, plastering a smile on my face for the usual round of meet and greet. The passengers appeared to be a pleasant lot, eager to visit the much acclaimed Caves of Diros. Since the majority were English it would make my day much easier. With 28 names ticked off my list, I was only waiting for Mr and Mrs Roberts to turn up: with only five minutes to anchors away, they were cutting it fine.

Feeling the sudden urge to make a call of nature, I found myself in a bit of bind. As the call became more urgent, I realised I would have to ask Milton to stand in for me with my clipboard whilst I made a dash for the loo. Fortunately, he was more than happy to make himself useful. My instruction to welcome the cutting it fine arrivals on-board and tick their names off the list wasn't too onerous even for Milton.

I cast the blame on Maria's *loukoumades* to explain my rather prolonged visit to the basic facilities. By the time I finally exited the head, Vasos had already steered the boat out to sea. Feeling deleterious in my duties, I was reassured when Milton reported that the Roberts had safely made it on board. Leaving Milton to sun himself in a corner of the deck, I made my way to the wheel house for one of my regular chats with Vasos before making my rounds.

Vasos was clearly full of the joys of spring, greeting me with a hearty, "Victor, I love you, beautiful towel." I began to suspect he was already hitting the ouzo until he announced, "*Tis spilies simera,*" indicating he was at least sober enough to know he needed to head for the caves. It would take a couple of hours to travel from town to Diros, Vasos following a southerly route. Unlike on the Lazy Day Cruise, the trip was full steam ahead to our destination, with a further stop for lunch once the caves had been fully explored. It was a perfect day for it, the sea calm and not a cloud in the sky.

Vasos kindly offered me a turn with his bin-oculars as the two of us gazed out to the horizon in companionable silence. Sami appeared on the top deck which backed onto the wheel house, slopping his mop across the glass in a desultory fashion. By the time he'd finished it was notice-ably filthier than when he'd started. Vasos la-mented that Sami just didn't have the same touch as Violet Burke when it came to cleaning the windscreen. I concurred, recalling she had indeed made it sparkle by giving it a vigorous rub with an *ouzo* soaked rag.

"*O Sami fainetei ligo kato,*" I said, observing that Sami seemed a bit down.

"*O Sami echei mia gyniaka apo ti Moldovia.*" Vasos confided that Sami had a woman from Moldova.

"Moldova," I repeated, trying to recall if the small impoverished nation was still under the choke of Communism. I must confess to being woefully ignorant about the state of affairs in the landlocked country, though I had recently read an interesting article in one of the Sundays about the breakaway Republic of Transnistria being rather embroiled in some sort of row over smuggled cigarettes and something else equally illicit that rather escaped me...chickens, that was it. Smuggled chickens.

Stroking his stubbly chin in a contemplative fashion, Vasos lowered his voice to tell me that he thought that the Moldovan woman was seeing Sami for his money. *"Nomizo oti i ygnaika tis Moldavias velpei ti Sami yia ta lefta tou."*

I was somewhat surprised to hear Vasos voice this opinion. I had rather presumed that the deckhand come dogsbody only earned a mere pittance. Perhaps I should enquire if slopping the mop around paid more than repping.

"Nomizo yia ta chrimata tou," Vasos said with a heavy sigh, repeating his thought that it was for the money.

"Nomizeis." My reply of 'you think' would have to suffice as I lacked the necessary Greek vocabulary to voice my actual thought of *she's hardly seeing Sami for his scintillating conversation.* I made a mental note to look up the Greek for scintillating and its relevant synonyms when I got home. One never knew when it would come in useful.

"Einai poly ftochoi sti Moldovia, ftochoteroi apo tous Alvanous," Vasos said. As I mentally translated that he had just told me they are very poor in Moldova, even poorer than the Albanians, I hoped for Sami's sake that he didn't become too

entangled. It was bad enough listening to Guzim constantly complain that his wife ate all of his money. Still, I supposed in Sami's case there would be no complaints to actually listen to since he is mute.

Vasos shared a few other details about the woman Sami had met, telling me that she was a cleaner in a local hotel. I thought that at least that gave them something in common, with the pair of them both slopping mops around for a living. I could see why Vasos may be worried she was a gold digger when he told me that she had a *kok* habit. Fortunately the bizarre misunderstanding that Sami had taken up with a cocaine user who fed her daily habit with regular trips to the bakery was soon sorted out when my handy Greek to English pocket dictionary revealed that a *kok* is also a chocolate doughnut. Mind you, a regular habit of chocolate doughnuts doesn't come cheap, as well as soon adding the pounds on the scales.

Telling Vasos that I must circulate amongst the tourists for a bit of chat, I left him to it. Noticing that Milton had fallen fast asleep, I worried that he would burn. Having only left home to pop up to Lidl, he was woefully unprepared to be exposed to the elements on the open sea.

Grabbing one of Vasos' grubby damp towels, I threw it over Milton's head to protect him from the sun, hoping that the pungent smell of stale sweat didn't rub off on him. It would make for a very unpleasant drive home later if it did.

Strolling around the deck, I took the time to stop and chat with the tourists, making small talk about where they were staying and if they were enjoying their holidays. I fobbed off a few questions about the caves, promising to go into more detail later: on the Diros trip, I prefer to save all the informative spiel about the caves until we are on the last leg of the approach to our destination. As I had come to expect, quite a few couples expressed an interest in my personal story of up-sticking to Greece, many of them envious of my life changing move. Many holiday-makers often shared that they wished they could follow suit, asking my advice about settling in a foreign country. For most of them with a 9 to 5 to return to, it was simply a pipe-dream, though quite a few were keen to find a holiday home in Greece.

As was my wont, I had learned to keep the name of my village to myself, simply revealing that I lived in a mountain area away from the coast. I would hate for Meli to become overrun with any British that I hadn't had chance to give a thorough vetting to first. Perish the thought that we would be invaded by the likes of Harold and Joan, installing swimming pools at the drop of a hat with nary a thought to the precarious water situation.

I was however mindful of Spiros' pressing need to sell the house he had inherited from his Uncle Leo. Urging me to try and drum up a buyer, he had offered me a generous commission if I could find him someone to flog it to. Spiros rather trusted my good judgement, knowing that I had a vested interest in being a tad fussy when it came to introducing potential new villagers into such a close-knit community. Considering my prospective cookery classes, my ideal buyer would be rather inept in the kitchen and wealthy enough to pay for lessons, without being so rich they would be tempted to sink a pool.

A woman of about my own age, dressed way over the top for a casual boat trip, sidled over to me. Long artificial nails scraped my skin as she placed a possessive hand on my arm: I cringed inwardly at the sight of her blood red talons, a particular vanity I find quite repellent. At the same time, my olfactory senses were

immediately overwhelmed by the overpowering perfume she had liberally applied; still it
worked to my advantage as she soon unlatched
herself when I succumbed to a bout of violent
sneezing triggered by her scent. Mentally running through the day's list of trippers, I recalled
that she had introduced herself during embar-
kation as Lucille, a gay divorcee holidaying with
her daughter and son-in-law.

"You must tell me all about living in Greece,
I'm sure it must be fascinating," she cooed.

"Not really," I said, playing it cool when I
spotted the predatory look in her eye. It was on
rare occasions such as this that I wished that Sa-
kis came along on the boat trips. The handsome
moustached Greek coach driver was the perfection distraction; next to him I didn't get a look
in. He was a real magnet for unattached women
fancying their own Shirley Valentine experience. "My wife and I lead a very quiet life over
here, just working and growing veggies, all terribly dull."

I could see Lucille visibly deflate at the mention of my wife, her eyes beginning to roam over
the other men in the group in the hope that one
of them may be unattached. Her gaze flitted dismissively over Milton; although he has quite a

distinguished if shabby air about him generally, he wasn't looking his best with Vasos' towel flung over his head. I could only imagine Lucille's reaction if she knew that he was the infamous Scarlett Bottom, though of course that would only impress her if she was an avid reader of porn: it was hardly the sort of thing one could casually ask. Spotting Vasos coming out of the toilet, I called him over in desperation before Lucille's hand could reattach itself to my arm.

"This is Captain Vasos. He owns this magnificent boat Pegasus, lovely fellow," I said.

"Hello, good, yes, beautiful," Vasos boomed, rattling his way through most of the English vocabulary he has mastered.

"Your own boat," Lucille gushed, batting her eyelashes nineteen to the dozen as I made my escape. It was fortunate that Sami had charge of the wheel since Vasos was now on a full charm offensive, Lucille eagerly lapping it up.

Having passed the time of day with most of the passengers, I made my way up the ladder to the upper deck. As my head drew level with the deck, I spotted a woman who looked all too familiar, a woman I had no desire at all to run into.

With my feet still firmly planted on the rungs, desperate thoughts of flight ran through my mind as I heard the woman cry out;

"Victor Bucket, well I never. Fancy seeing you here."

Chapter 22

A Blast from the Past

The unwelcome words rang in my ears as I hastily legged it back down the ladder in the desperate but futile hope that this blast from the past was nothing more than a bad dream. The moment my feet touched solid ground, a blonde head appeared above me, peering over the railing. Realising that if I backed up anymore, I may end up as the proverbial man overboard, I resigned myself to the inevitable, saying, "Hello, Kimberly. What on earth are you doing here?"

V.D. BUCKET

Perhaps you are wondering how I know Kimberly. She was Barry's first wife, the one he was married to before he divorced her.

When I asked my former sister-in-law what she was doing here, I genuinely wanted to know how she had managed to sneak on-board Pegasus without my spotting her at the gangplank. With a sinking feeling, I recalled handing my clipboard to Milton earlier when I answered a call of nature. There had only been one pair of stragglers still left to board: the Roberts. It didn't take a genius to work out that Kimberly must be one half of that couple. At least she wasn't casting a blight on Barry's surname any more.

"I'm on my holidays. What a funny coincidence that you are holidaying in the same place. I suppose Marigold is with you," Kimberly called down. Her voice hadn't mellowed with the passage of time even though it was a good decade since I'd had the misfortune to run into her; it still carried the distinctive sound of nails being scraped on a chalkboard. I reflected that Kimberly had always been a bit on the dim side and things clearly hadn't improved. Even though she was staring at me intently, she apparently hadn't twigged that I was kitted out in a holiday rep's uniform. I wondered if she supposed that I was so sartorially challenged that I would choose to walk round in a flame resistant modacrylic polo shirt emblazoned with a large Greek flag, complete with a whistle draped round my neck. Surely it was obvious that I wouldn't be caught dead in such an outfit if the holiday company didn't dictate that I wear it.

The next thing I knew, a pair of legs descended the ladder with a slight wobble and I found myself nose to nose with Barry's ex, the woman who practically dragged him up the aisle kicking and screaming. Barry always was too good natured for his own good and when Kimberly got it into her head that he'd proposed, he insisted the decent thing was to go through with it. As Marigold never failed to point out, they were terribly unsuited from the off, Kimberly having ambitions for the finer things in life whilst Barry has always been solidly down to earth. Kimberly would never have managed to drag Barry away on something as exotic as a package holiday to Greece, my brother-in-law always being content with a week in a caravan in Colwyn Bay or Rhyl. Until Marigold and I moved to Greece, Barry had never as much as left England; well, apart from his trips to Wales.

"I can't get over you holidaying in the same place," Kimberly trilled. "Are you here for a week or a fortnight?"

"A bit longer than that," I admitted, my brain racing out of control like a washing machine stuck on the spin cycle. If Kimberley was genuinely on her holidays, perhaps she hadn't tracked Barry down to Greece as I had initially feared. I attempted to present a calm demeanour, girding myself to be grilled at any moment. Knowing Kimberly, she would be desperate to vacuum up whatever information she could about Barry.

My brother-in-law was never one to rake over the details of his failed marriage, though he had of course confided that Kimberly refused to accept that their marriage was over even after Barry moved out. I recalled that she often turned up on our doorstep in floods of tears in a desperate attempt to appeal to Marigold's good nature to talk some sense into her brother. Naturally, Marigold took Barry's side. Where necessary, Marigold resorted to a spot of manipulation, telling Kimberly that she was far too good for Barry. Marigold wasn't above reminding Kimberly about certain nasty habits of Barry's that drove Kimberly up the wall, such as his re-volting penchant for bringing tripe home on a regular basis. I recalled that she had spent most of her time nagging Barry to do things that he had no interest in, preferring a quiet life. He is much the same now, content to potter round Meli, oblivious to the outside world.

"Fancy running into you here," I said, try-ing to buy time until my thoughts were less scrambled. "Are you remarried now?" I asked, having guessed that her surname had changed to Roberts.

"Yes, I married again," she said. Looking up, she shrieked "Malcolm" at the top of her voice. A hen pecked looking chap with a nasty case of sunburn dutifully stuck his head above the railings. Kimberly called up, "Talk about co-incidences, Victor here is on holiday at the same time as us and he's from Manchester too."

Just at that moment Lucille sidled up next to me, her taloned hand once again settling posses-sively on my arm. Her interruption was timely. "Oh, your Captain is such a gentleman and so complimentary. Do you think you can fix it so that I could sit next to him at lunch?"

"I'll certainly see what I can do," I prom-ised. Since Lucille was female and had a pulse, I couldn't see Vasos raising any objections.

"I ticked the chicken as the lunch menu option. I'm almost certain that the Fray Bentos pie the Captain was talking about wasn't an option. Fancy them serving that in Greece…"

"Perhaps you could relay a message to the Captain for me. Tell him I'd like the Fray Bentos option too," I said in a desperate attempt to get rid of Lucille; she was most definitely giving Kimberly the wrong impression.

As Lucille rushed off to re-engage with Vasos, Kimberly arched her meticulously plucked eyebrows and narrowed her eyes. "Does Marigold know about her? I thought that she kept you on a tight rein?"

"I'm not a horse, Kimberly," I said, snapping her down.

"Of course not, sorry. And Barry?" she hissed, lowering her voice presumably so that husband number two wouldn't catch on as she got to the crunch.

"Oh, you know Barry. He never changes, same old stick-in-the-mud," I said, hoping to remind her that she'd found Barry so dull that she was constantly trying to change him. Realising that I was woefully ill-prepared to deal with this tricky predicament, I clutched my stomach and excused myself by declaring that I must answer a call of nature. Since it struck me that the best course of action would be to take advice from my good lady wife, I locked myself in the toilet and dialled our number from my mobile.

"We're just on our way out, dear," Marigold said as soon as she answered. "Ashley is taking us for a drive in his hire car…"

"Never mind that now. I'm calling about a more pressing matter. Kimberly is on the boat…"

"Kimberly?"

"Barry's ex…"

"Don't tell me that mad harpy has tracked him down to Greece."

"No, she doesn't seem to have a clue that he's here, she's on her holidays with Barry's replacement. What should I do?"

"Well, whatever you do, don't let on that Barry is living over here. You know that he doesn't want to have anything to do with Kimberly…and can you imagine Cynthia's reaction if Kimberly turned up in Meli? She wouldn't be happy."

"That's an understatement to say the least. Kimberly seems to think that I'm on my holidays."

"In that ridiculous uniform," Marigold guffawed. "Well, she never was very bright but I'm sure that even Kimberly will cotton on that you're working as a tour guide when you eventually get round to doing some actual work. Is that imminent?"

"Yes, we'll be at the caves soon and I must deliver my spiel before we arrive."

"Then if you must, tell her that we live in Greece, but for heaven's sake don't give her our address. Fob her off with some story about us heading to Athens later today for a mini-break to ensure we avoid her...and don't breathe a word about Barry being over here."

The rattling of the toilet door was followed by some impatient banging.

"I have to go..." I said, cutting the call short and reluctantly opening the door a crack.

"I say, old chap, do you think it was that pie that you ate? Or perhaps a delayed contaminated reaction from being stuck in the bins?" Milton asked.

"What?"

"Well, it's the second time that you've disappeared in the head for a frightfully long time. I was worried that you've come down with a dicky tummy..."

Before Milton could complete his sentence, I grabbed him by the shirt front and pulled him into the toilet. It had suddenly occurred to me that my neighbour's loose lips could land me in it unless I primed him in advance.

"Milton, I need you to do something for me."

"Anything, old chap. Just say the word."

"It's a bit delicate. It turns out that Barry's ex-wife is on this trip but she doesn't have a clue that Barry has moved to Greece…"

Tapping the side of his nose knowingly, Milton said, "Ah, got you, old chap. Mum's the word and all that. Barry's whereabouts will remain as much as a mystery as Scarlett Bottom's. I'll go one better, never even heard of him, news to me that Marigold has a brother."

"Thank you Milton, your discretion is much appreciated," I said as we exited the head, attracting a raised eyebrow from Captain Vasos and Lucille who were standing outside, deep in a meaningless exchange about beautiful towels.

As Pegasus sailed the last stretch of sea towards our destination, I gathered my charges together to deliver my well-practised spiel, hoping that Kimberly's presence didn't throw me off course.

V.D. BUCKET

I began by informing my party that Diros is re-
garded as one of the most spectacular caves in
the world and that although the site dates back
to the Neolithic Age, the caves of Vlychada and
Alepotripa had only been discovered in 1958
and as yet only Vlychada had been opened for
exploration, Alepotripa still inaccessible. I explained that they would explore the intricate
passageways and chambers in small boats
which would carry them along the subterranean
Glyfada River. The network of passages would
be dimly lit, allowing them to marvel at the impressive stalagmites and stalactites in all their
natural beauty.

I imparted the interesting fact that the fos-
silised bones of a hippopotamus had been discovered in the cave of Vlychada, following this
detail with a witty quip that one doesn't expect
to trip over many hippos in Greece. My little
joke was well received with a suitable amount
of laughter, though Milton rather stole my thun-
der by piping up, "Aggressive creatures what,
always falling over damn hippopotami back in
Kenya."

Hastily interrupting Milton before he could
derail my talk, I told the group that evidence indicated the caves were once used as a burial site

and that skeletons had been discovered, ensuring my words were suitably dramatic. Almost as one, my party engaged in a collective shiver, a natural reaction despite the sun shining down on them. I elaborated by telling them that the evidence of the caves having once been inhabited was borne out with additional discoveries of tools, pottery and jewellery.

"You may find the cool temperatures underground a welcome relief from the sun, but do grab a cardie if you don't fancy the chill. Now, we will be exploring in small boats which seat up to eight. Do please put your life-jackets on before entering the boats: I would hate to lose any of you to a watery grave. Also please remember to keep your heads down especially in low passages and try not to wobble the boats. The boats will be poled through the water..."

Mr Meadows raised his arm as though in the classroom, interrupting my spiel with a question. There's always one.

"No don't, worry Mr Meadows, you won't have to do it yourselves, there are professional guides..."

Another inane question broke my flow.

"Yes, quite, that does indeed allow you to concentrate on ducking if necessary. No really, no need to worry, Mr Meadows. As you can see, I'm six feet tall myself and the top of my head is still intact even though I've been in the caves many times. Now, as I was saying, the passageways lead into a freshwater lake…"

Another interruption; this was becoming repetitive.

"No, I wouldn't recommend that you actually drink from it, one can't really say how long the water has been standing or what previous tourists may have dropped in it. It could be dreadfully unhygienic."

Skilfully ignoring Mr Meadow's raised hand, I delivered the rest of my spiel just in time for Vasos to manoeuvre Pegasus to the pier. The excitement amongst the group was palpable, everyone eager to explore the caves in the expectation that it would be the highlight of their holiday in Greece. Shutting off the engine, Vasos hurried to join me on the gangplank to offer a steadying hand to the tourists as they disembarked, making them laugh as he dropped in a regular dose of "beautiful," "good," "hello," "I love you," and "towel." Feeling a tad guilty at the prospect of leaving Vasos alone on the boat to be shouted at by Milton, I steered the latter towards the coffee shop so that he could wait in the shade. Unfortunately, I couldn't sneak non-paying passengers inside the main attraction and I had no intention of coughing up for his ticket.

Kimberly caught up with me as we made our way up the steep path to the entrance to the caves.

"Fancy you working over here, Victor?" she panted, having finally cottoned on to the fact that I was the tour guide. "I suppose that all those germs must have got too much for you. I know that I could never face a duck in orange sauce again after that horrendous tale you recounted...and in a supposedly five star hotel too. Victor, I need to ask you a favour."

Here it comes, I thought to myself. *Time to get inventive with the truth.*

"I'd really rather you didn't mention Barry in front of Malcolm. He can get wildly jealous whenever his name is brought up. He just hates the thought of my having been married before."

Even as I exhaled in relief, I was annoyed that I had spent the better part of my morning expending energy worrying about something which apparently wasn't going to rear its ugly head after all.

Chapter 23

Befuddled Grandfathers

The tour of the caves was a resounding success, none of my charges falling out of the boats or bashing their heads to a bloody pulp on the low passages, though Mr Meadows did manage to put an unsightly dent in the top of his jaunty straw boater. The silence of the caves was only broken by the collective gasps of awe at the magnificent grandeur of the prehistoric stalactites suspended from the vaulted ceilings, their reflected colours shimmering in the water, and the echoed plop of the paddles as the boatmen punted us through the dimly lit waterways towards the subterranean lake.

Back on Pegasus, everyone exclaimed about the wonderful experience, describing it as splendid, fabulous, amazing and serene. Unless something untoward happened over lunch, I was confident that the customer satisfaction surveys would be full of glowing praise. I felt quite sorry for Milton having missed out on the caves but he assured me that it wasn't a loss at all as he tended to be a tad claustrophobic.

Since Lucille rather monopolised Vasos over lunch, to his great delight, I found myself stuck with Milton and the ever silent Sami. Fortunately, Kimberly kept her distance, although she did keep glancing over in my direction. I imagine that she was eager to grill me about Barry if only her over jealous husband would relinquish his tight rein: an ironic touch which I relished in light of her earlier comment about Marigold keeping me under control. Milton earned his keep by reporting back, after a visit to the taverna toilet, that he had overheard Mr Roberts griping about being dragged to Greece. Apparently he would have been quite content with a week in Blackpool; the Greek heat didn't suit him at all, his sunburn was painful and he was terribly wary of eating foreign food.

I was delighted when Pegasus docked in town without incident. I had managed to keep well away from Kimberly on the return journey by utilising a bit of nifty footwork whenever I sensed her approach. After disembarking with her husband, Kimberly used the pathetic excuse of leaving her towel on-board to sneak back on to attempt to grill me about Barry. Instead of satisfying her curiosity, I simply handed over her towel while remarking that her husband was eyeing us jealously and would likely get the wrong idea and jump to the conclusion that something was going on between the pair of us. In truth, Mr Roberts, a most innocuous looking fellow who looked totally bored, was merely squinting in the sunlight rather than eyeing us with anything even approaching jealousy. Still, no doubt it kept Kimberly feeling self-important to imagine her second husband was the possessive type.

A middle-aged woman of rather unremarkable appearance cut a solitary figure waiting on the quayside, huddled inside an anorak. I doubt I would have noticed her if it wasn't for the way that she was staring wistfully at the sea.

Perchance she was waiting hopelessly for the return of a lost love that had sailed away. She rather put me in mind of Puccini's Madame Butterfly pining for the return of Pinkerton, though the drab anorak didn't have the same romantic appeal as a kimono. As I mulled her story, I was taken aback when Sami practically vaulted the gang-plank; rushing over to the woman with an uncharacteristic speed of movement, he folded her in a tender embrace.

"Love," Vasos boomed, confirming the woman's identity as Sami's Moldovan woman. It rather cheered me up to think that her wait hadn't been in vain.

After making a rather rash promise that I would most definitely get together with *Kapetanios* Vasos over the course of the winter for a night of carousing and debauchery, I made my way to the tour office, instructing Milton to wait out of sight until I had turned my whistle in to Cynthia. I was happy to hang it up until the start of the next tourist season.

"How did it go?" Cynthia asked.

"I think we'll see positive scores on the customer satisfaction surveys," I replied.

"Marigold mentioned that you were popping into Lidl on your way home," Cynthia said.

"Yes indeed, but I have a spot of shopping to do in town first. I want to buy a pair of boat shoes."

Ever since noticing how completely ridiculous Ashley looked sporting socks paired with sandals, I had decided to invest in a personal style makeover. Nothing too drastic of course since a smart button down and tie is my signature style, but a change of footwear was most definitely in order. The sandals would still get a wearing on sockless occasions, but for more formal wear I would replace them with a nice pair of suede boat shoes. Marigold would no doubt be delighted to be finally rid of my socks and sandals combo; she never fails to drop derogatory comments whenever they get an airing. I believe the term, "You look like a real plonker," may have passed her lips on more than one occasion.

"You may have to give the shoes a miss. All the shops are closed until evening for the siesta. Still, you might luck out and find a pair in Lidl."

"Perish the thought. I hardly think that anything stylish will come from a cut-price supermarket."

"I managed to find someone to cover your final excursion next week. I think it's marvellous the way that you've stepped up to help Tina out at the shop, such community spirit," Cynthia gushed. "That reminds me, would you buy some nappies for Anastasia in Lidl? I've jotted down what I need. Tina's prices are quite outrageous."

"Anything for my gorgeous niece," I agreed.

"Thank you, Victor. I'll be stuck here for another few hours with paperwork."

"I'll drop the nappies off with Barry when I get back to Meli."

Heading back to the car, I suddenly remembered Milton. Much as I was tempted to drive off without him, I did the decent thing and bundled him into the passenger seat. It had completely slipped my mind about most of the shops closing until Cynthia reminded me, so putting my foot down we headed straight off to Lidl; being of German extraction, the chain flouted the Greek habit of siestas. I must confess to feeling a tad apprehensive about purchasing Cynthia's supplies: it was almost four decades since Benjamin was in nappies and back then it was all terry towelling rather than disposable. It struck me that with the way Cynthia is forever banging on about all things ecological, she ought to take a leaf out of the way we used to do things. Perchance Doreen could be persuaded to knock up a line of washable nappies from Marigold's old curtains and soft furnishings.

Since I am not joined at the hip with Milton, I made the suggestion that we each steer separate trolleys around the store and meet at the tills. This was indeed a propitious move since I chanced upon a bargain bin full of boat shoes: it wouldn't have done my image any good to have Milton's loose lips blabbing that I decked my feet out in Lidl's finest. The disadvantage of buying shoes in a supermarket rather than a shoe shop soon became apparent when I attempted to try a suitable looking pair on, only to discover that both shoes were attached firmly together by their laces. Scoping the aisle out to check that I was unobserved, I slipped my feet into the shoes, almost falling flat on my face when I tried to test them out for comfort. Shuffling forward in two tied together shoes with barely an inch between them does not provide the optimum shopping experience. Nevertheless, I threw my find into the trolley, secreting them below a couple of giant packets of toilet rolls. I had no intention of paying Tina's outrageous prices and had clean forgotten to ask if she would be offering me a managerial discount.

Milton popped up by my side pushing a trolley laden down with cases of tinned cat food that was on offer. Since it was such a bargain, I threw a few cases in too, hoping that Marigold's domestics would not turn their noses up at my choice: I didn't recognise it as a brand that my wife had ever personally taste tested in her line of employ. Milton and I ended up looking like a pair of helpless saps in the baby product aisle. Between the two of us, neither of us could fathom out the mystery of disposable nappies.

Fortunately a very pleasant young Greek woman with a toddler of her own noticed that we were floundering out of our depth. As she came to our rescue piling the correct size of disposable nappies into my trolley, she cooed to her child, *"Prepei na voithiso aftous tous dyo pappoudes pou einai safos berdemenoi."* I didn't bother translating her words for Milton's benefit: he didn't need to know that she said she must help these two grandfathers who were clearly befuddled.

Two trolleys full of extremely bulky purchases presented us with a real dilemma when we returned to the Punto. The boot was practically full with deckchairs and other beach paraphernalia which had been left in the car. There was nothing for it but to pile cases of wine and cat food, and giant packets of loo rolls and nappies, on the back seat. Even with our purchases piled so high that they obscured the back window, we still had an odd case of cat food that we couldn't cram into the car. The only solution was to drive home with Milton perched on a case of cat food on the passenger seat. There would be no stopping for any ancient hitchhikers who waved me down with their walking sticks today. There wasn't even any room left to stuff in a very nimble Greek pensioner.

"Spiffing day out, what," Milton enthused as we crawled out of the car park, my fingers crossed that the laden down Punto would make it up the mountain. "I must say your Captain friend is a real character, though between you and me, I found it a bit unnerving the way he kept declaring that he loved me. Still, should give Edna a laugh to think I've still got it. Not many men of my age with a dodgy hip can say that."

Chapter 24

A Very Human Side

After bracing myself to put on a show of politeness in front of our house-guests, I was elated to discover no sign of them when I returned home. Marigold was cooing over Anastasia in the grand salon, the baby gurgling with pleasure when I rushed over to scoop her up for a cuddle. After being stuck in the car with Milton for what seemed like eternity, a bunch of sticky kisses from my adorable niece was just the tonic I needed.

"Can you believe that Cynthia tasked me with buying disposable nappies for this cute little bundle? It was all a tad confusing when I think back to how simple things were with Benjamin," I said, contorting my features into outlandish expressions to amuse little Ana. My distorted efforts were not in vain, the baby clapping her hands with glee at my absurd performance.

"I think I'd take disposable over a bucket of soiled towelling. One can't help but notice though that Cynthia is only environmentally friendly when it suits," Marigold said rather cattily.

"Now, darling, she's definitely an improvement on the last wife...did you mention anything about Kimberly turning up in Greece when Barry dropped the baby off?"

"No, I didn't want to air his dirty laundry in front of Geraldine and Ashley."

"Where are they?"

"They popped out for a stroll around the village. I'm afraid that I dropped a few none-too-subtle hints that I fancied a bit of alone time when we returned from our day out," Marigold confessed. "If I wasn't looking after Anastasia, I would be more than tempted to pour myself a large brandy to steady my nerves."

"Has something unsettled you, dear?" I asked in concern.

"Ashley's driving. It certainly leaves a lot to be desired. He's worse than the Greeks behind the wheel, and that's saying something. I was a bag of gibbering nerves by the time we got home."

"You surprise me. Somehow I can't imagine Ashley tearing through the streets as though he's at Brands Hatch."

"Oh no, it was quite the opposite." I could swear Marigold's eyes did a 360 degree swivel beneath her raised eyebrows. "He drove at such a crawl that he was a public menace, he wouldn't even overtake a pushbike. The cyclist appeared quite unnerved, wobbling all over the place. Ashley deliberately hogged the central white lines to prevent anyone from overtaking. I tell you, Victor, it was no joke being tailgated by Panos' tractor. I swear I could almost feel the slobber from that huge ferocious guard dog of his hitting the back of my neck."

I cringed in sympathy. Exceedingly slow drivers are indeed a menace, though generally more of a nuisance during the height of summer when they descend on the Mani en masse. Self-absorbed oblivious tourists dawdling along with their cameras at the ready, and camper vans travelling in slow motion convoys, can be an accident waiting to happen: local folks going about their everyday business are easily tempted to take unnecessary and dangerous risks to pass them. As we approached our two-year anniversary of living in Greece, I was becoming acclimatised to Greek drivers and wary of any vehicle displaying a hire sticker.

"Did you go anywhere nice?" I asked.

"We popped down to the coast for a spot of lunch and then a swim. Apart from when he was behind the wheel, Ashley was like a new man compared to yesterday evening. He was most attentive to Geraldine and he acted like a complete gentleman over lunch, I was beginning to see his human side..."

"He has a human side," I scoffed. "That's a bit of a turn-up for the books."

"I was starting to think that we'd judged him a bit hastily but then when Geraldine wanted him to join us in the sea for a swim he turned all sniffy again."

"How so?"

"He preferred to park himself on a seafront bench with his nose stuck in one of his boring books rather than joining us for a dip."

"Perhaps he was embarrassed to expose his body in a pair of swimming trunks," I suggested. "He's hardly got the physique for it."

"That's putting it mildly. His refusal to swim put rather a damper on things for Geraldine. I rather think she may have hoped that Ashley would be attracted to her in her bathing costume. Once we were in the sea and out of earshot, she told me that he's forever blowing hot and cold, and of course I've seen it for myself now. The poor dear has no idea where she stands with Ashley," Marigold sighed. "I just hope that no one we know saw me out and about with him. I was mortified when I saw what he was reading. He made no attempt to hide the title of his book...how he could even think of reading it in a public place."

"Something on mould," I said hopefully.

"I wish. Anything would have been preferable to some dreary treatise entitled 'Genital Herpes.'" Marigold's last two words were whispered in deference to the delicate ears of our baby niece. "Even from the sea, I could see passersby balking as they clocked the title."

"And to think that I was of the opinion that anyone reading Milton's 'Delicious Desire' should conceal it in a brown paper wrapping," I quipped. "It's really quite mild in the scheme of objectionable reading matter."

"It's just a good job that Ashley can't speak Greek or I'd never have let him wander off around Meli without supervision. He'd most likely be stopping the villagers to interrogate them about any sexually transmitted infections they'd ever picked up."

"Quite," I agreed, appreciating the way Marigold avoided using the triggering term venereal disease. She is always so empathetic when it comes to my personal sensitivities.

Our concerns about Ashley were forgotten in a flash when Anastasia began to bawl inconsolably, pulling at her bottom lip and dribbling rather messily.

"Whatever's the matter, sweetheart? Tell Aunty Marigold so I can make everything better," Marigold cooed.

"The baby is only seven months old, how do you expect her to tell you what's upset her?" I pointed out, rushing over to wipe up Anastasia's drool with a tissue. Something green was caught in the strand of dribbled saliva. As I captured it on the tissue, I realised to my horror that it was a green shield bug; it must have flown into the baby's open mouth. It was no wonder that she was screaming like a banshee. The flying insects are not known as green stink bugs for nothing, their smell being particularly vile. I was forever reminding Marigold not to squash them as it releases their foul smelling secretions, the odour lingering like a bad smell, for want of better wording. Although I have never encountered the scent of a skunk, I imagine it is quite pleasantly perfumed in comparison to that of the dreaded shield bugs which plague our lives from September onwards. The thought of one landing in little Ana's mouth didn't bear thinking about.

"Do squash it, Victor," Marigold instructed, the colour draining from her face when she realised Anastasia had very nearly swallowed the nasty thing.

"How many times do I need to tell you that squashing them only makes the smell ten times worse? You need to get in the habit of flushing them down the loo or releasing them from the balcony," I reminded my wife who was busy soothing the baby by force feeding her a square of orange cake to counter the disgusting taste in her mouth.

"We must take a trip to Lefteris' garden centre

and see if he has anything to deter them from coming indoors," Marigold declared, always up for a visit to the establishment run by the tattooed, leather clad young man with the pampered pet poodle, Fufu, who we had first encountered in the veterinarian's waiting room. Lefteris never fails to charm my wife; she can be a bit of a sucker for an attentive younger man turning on the flattery.

"It would be cheaper to sit in the dark. You know that the light attracts them," I suggested, making a feeble attempt at humour.

"Very droll. We do enough sitting round in the dark when the power goes off," Marigold reminded me. "Do you want to drop Anastasia back home with Barry? I want to get ready for this evening."

"This evening. What have you got in mind?"

"I thought we could take our guests to the taverna. Ashley is quite keen to eat organic after the way you raved about it."

"I suppose if we must put up with him, it will be preferable to dilute his presence in mixed company. I will do my best to persuade Barry to join us."

"Oh yes, do try. You can break the bad news

to him that Kimberly is in Greece without getting Cynthia's back up. She's working late so you can have a private word with Barry; warn him to keep to the village until Kimberly is safely stowed on a flight back to Manchester."

"Yes, dear." I might have known that I'd be the one lumbered with the unpleasant task of raking up Barry's past.

"Then both of you can bring the baby along to the taverna and meet us there. You know how Dina loves to make a huge fuss of little Ana."

"Just let me get out of my uniform and then I'll pop over to Barry's," I promised.

"Well do get a move on," Marigold urged impatiently. If I didn't know better, I would say she that was trying to get rid of me.

Never one to beat about the bush, I voiced my thought. "You seem awfully keen to get rid of me."

"I invited Luljeta up for a cup of tea; I can't help feeling sorry for her. You'd be terribly bored with our girlie chat."

"And did your invitation extend to Guzim?"

"Don't be silly, dear. He needs to muck out your chickens."

I was just leaving the house with Anastasia

when Marigold asked me to wait. Staring at me intently, she said, "I can't put my finger on it, but there's something different about you this evening, Victor."

"I can't think of anything," I said breezily dropping a kiss on her forehead as I left.

It would amuse me to keep Marigold guessing. Considering the amount of times she had complained about my pairing socks with sandals, one would have thought that it would be glaringly obvious that I was kitted out in my new boat shoes rather than sandals.

As I wheeled the baby back to Barry's, I ran into Geraldine and Ashley on their way back to our house.

"You go up, Geraldine. I'd like a quiet word with Victor," Ashley pronounced rather ominously. Granted, ominously may be a bit of an exaggeration but he definitely had a serious look on his face. In contrast, I could barely keep my face straight.

Although the light was beginning to fade, I could swear that Ashley's hair had changed colour again since this morning, morphing back from mousy to its original glossy dark brown. Perchance my imagination had gone into

overdrive earlier, supposing Ashley was sporting a wig. Perhaps in the honeyed hangover
state I'd been in from eating too many *loukoumades*, I had simply made a mistake or been
tricked by the light. Drawing closer to Ashley, I
studied his thatch. There was no denying that
the straggly hairs that had covered his ears this
morning had now disappeared, razor sharp
contouring once again accentuating his protruding ears. Even after giving him the benefit of the
doubt, there was no denying he was sporting an
artificial hairpiece. It struck me that he could
hardly intend to keep it a secret considering his
frequent switches between styles. I was very
tempted to scoop Anastasia out of her pram and
encourage her to get her hands on it. One good
yank should prove my point. Before I could put
my plan into action, I noticed that the baby was
dozing comfortably in her pram.

"I have to say, your words this morning..."
Ashley paused, his Adam's apple bulging in his
throat as he visibly gulped.

"A tad harsh, perhaps," I suggested, recalling that I hadn't been in the best of temper
when I'd lectured him about treating Geraldine
better.

"Quite the contrary, your words rather played

on my mind. The more that I mulled them over, the more they resonated with me. I feel quite ashamed to confess that you were right. I have indeed treated Geraldine in a most deplorable manner, or as you put it, in a shabby way."

"Well, if memory serves me correctly, you dismissed her as lazy and cloying," I reminded him. "It's hardly a ringing endorsement of true love."

"Just after you left this morning, Marigold asked me to pop over to the village shop for some milk," Ashley said. "I was surprised to see Geraldine confabbing with the local cleric in the church vestibule. I didn't disturb them but it struck me what a lovely person Geraldine is to take the time to visit the church even on holiday. I expect she was making a donation."

I almost choked on my effort to suppress an involuntary snort upon hearing Ashley's interpretation of what Geraldine was likely up to with Papas Andreas.

"You may be remiss if you allow such a good and charitable woman as Geraldine to slip through your fingers," I advised, thinking *charitable indeed*.

"Would you believe that I have actually grown quite fond of Geraldine?" Ashley continued.

"Though I do believe we may have rushed things by holidaying together so soon. We have only been seeing one another for just over three months. Fifteen weeks and four days to be exact."

"Well neither of you are exactly spring chickens so there's no point in hanging about. I married Marigold within five months of meeting her," I said. Out of deference to Marigold, I neglected to mention that it had been a shotgun wedding, though of course I would have married her anyway. "When you meet the one, you know it."

"But do you? I thought I'd met the one as you put it but she stood me up at the altar." Ashley averted his eyes in embarrassment as he spoke. Nervously tracing one earlobe with a finger and scratching an enormous mosquito bite on his forehead, he came perilously close to dislodging his hair piece.

"I'd no idea," I gasped, feeling a spark of sympathy. Being ditched on one's wedding day must be the most terrible humiliation, not easily overcome.

"It's not something I ever talk about. It took a decade to get over it. Naturally when I met Geraldine, I felt the need to move slowly rather than rush into things this time around."

"So you haven't shared this with Geraldine?"

"No, I don't want her to look at me as someone to be pitied."

"Better that she knows the truth. It's no wonder that she thinks that you've been blowing hot and cold…"

"I can't help myself. Each time I feel myself drawing closer to her, I am compelled to take a step back and put up my guard. I'm really a bit clueless how to act in matters of the heart. I couldn't face a second rejection," Ashley confided.

"Is Geraldine the first woman that you have dated since your unfortunate experience?"

"Yes, my love life has been a wasteland since I was publicaly jilted. And as things had moved along so quickly with Christine…" Ashley visibly shivered as he uttered the name of his ex, "I really don't want history to repeat itself."

Sensing there was more to Ashley's story, I encouraged him to get it off his chest. "You may as well tell me everything; you have my assurance that I won't repeat it, not even to Marigold. I'd hazard a guess that you may find that once you have confided in me, it will be easier for you to come clean to Geraldine, if you so choose."

Ashley hesitated before speaking. "Although I have never been one to rush things, I proposed to Christine after just two years of dating. I confess to feeling something like excitement when she accepted. I cannot begin to describe the mortification I felt on my wedding day when the vicar announced there was a phone call for me in the vestry. It was Christine saying that the wedding was off; she couldn't go through with it. She couldn't face tying herself down with someone as dull as me. To rub salt in the wound, she informed me that she had taken a lover."

I winced at her cruelty, thinking surely she must have cottoned on that Ashley was dull before she accepted his proposal. Ashley continued to speak and his sorry saga only got worse.

"As a parting shot, Christine advised me to get myself checked out at the VD clinic. It turned out that not only had she been two-timing me, she'd infected me with a nasty dose of gonorrhoea. After that, I found it impossible to trust again."

"I would have presumed that a man in your line of work would have taken sensible precautions…"

"I didn't make a career out of VD until I was personally afflicted."

"So, I suppose, in one manner of speaking, something good came out of being publically dumped."

"When you put it like that, I think you're right. If I'd never been ditched at the altar, I'd never have got into VD and it's a very satisfying line to be in."

"It's no wonder you were so cautious about jumping into bed with Geraldine…"

"Perhaps I will take your advice and tell Geraldine everything. Do you suppose that if she knew the truth, she'd be willing to be patient with me?" Ashley asked, his voice betraying a natural hesitancy.

"I expect so, but don't leave her hanging too long. All she wants is to be married and settled but if you leave her dangling she may just turn to the church for comfort," I warned.

Chapter 25

A Very Bad Business

Strolling towards Barry's house with the pram, I must confess to feeling a certain smugness, confident that I had successfully steered the relationship between Ashley and Geraldine in a new, more hopeful, direction. Since Ashley had revealed that he was indeed human, I was willing to give him a second chance, providing I could persuade him to stop bleating on about venereal diseases.

A gurgle from Anastasia alerted me that she was awake. Leaning over to adjust her cotton sunhat, I cooed, "Your Aunty Marigold will be tickled pink if she ever hears about my match-making."

Of course, I was aware that Marigold would remain oblivious unless Ashley ever revealed that I had stuck my oar in; I had given him my word that I wouldn't blab. Spilling the beans to Anastasia didn't count since she was incapable of repeating it.

I found Barry perched on a sun lounger by the ecological pond, glass in hand, serenaded by the croak of frogs. Barry reeked of the vinegar he had splashed on to repel the flying insects and mosquitoes that are drawn to the water in early evening. The colour of the blue irises in the pond appeared to flit between lilac and purple shades as the nebulous glow of the setting sun reflected on the water. I watched in fascination as a frog sprang into motion; pouncing on a spider spinning its web amidst the leafy vegetation, it devoured its prey, its bulging eyes blinking rapidly as the tasty snack went down.

After pouring me a glass of wine, Barry bounced the baby on his knee and started to fill me in on progress on the *apothiki*.

"Never mind that now, Barry. There's something I must tell you before Cynthia gets back."

"If you're going to complain that she was lording it over you in the office, I don't want to hear it. You can't expect me to take sides between my wife and my brother."

I was touched beyond measure by Barry's casual choice of words; it warmed the cockles of my heart to hear him drop the in-law suffix and refer to me as his brother.

"It's nothing to do with work, well only loosely. Kimberly was on Pegasus today for the Caves of Diros tour," I revealed.

"Kimberly. How on earth did she find out that I'm in Greece?" Barry groaned, automatically assuming that his first wife had tracked him down. His assumption was not unrealistic since Kimberly had always been persistent in pursuing Barry even after their marriage broke down.

"She hasn't..." I spluttered, slinging the contents of my glass to the ground in disgust. "Good grief, Barry, this wine has turned, it tastes like rancid vinegar."

"Oh sorry, Victor, I poured you a glass from my bottle of vinegar and honey. I developed quite a taste for it and I never suffer from car sickness if I take glass regularly," Barry said. "What's this about Kimberly, then?"

"She's out here on a package holiday. Fortunately she has husband number two with her…"

"Some other poor sod has married her?"

"Yes, there's no accounting for taste."

"Blimey, she may have bought the tickets from Cynthia. They could have run into one another without even realising it."

"You're right. That thought never even occurred to me. It looks like you dodged a bullet there."

Exchanging glances, we exhaled our relief in unison.

"Anyway, I was able to keep Kimberly at arm's length and I managed to fob her off when she asked about you. She's no idea that you're living over here, or married with a baby. Just make sure that you stick to the village until she flies back to Manchester at the weekend, it would be terrible if you ran into her in one of the tourist spots."

"I appreciate the heads up. I have an appointment on the coast at noon tomorrow to give a quote to a British couple who want some work doing once we're finished with your *apothiki*. I'll get Vangelis to go down instead. It would be just my luck to run into Kimberly." Covering Anastasia's ears with his hands, Barry hissed, "Not a word to Cynthia; you probably haven't noticed but she can get a bit jealous."

"Mum's the word," I promised. It struck me that Cynthia's green-eyed tendency was entirely misplaced. Barry hadn't expressed the slightest interest in Kimberly, not even enquiring how she was looking. Having happily moved on with his life, Barry had no interest in digging up the past. Still, as Cynthia was capable of working herself into a tizzy over Barry's harmless flirtation with the elderly Litsa, she would most likely have a fit of the screaming habdabs if she got wind of Kimberly.

"How are you getting on with your house-guests?" Barry asked. "I imagine Geraldine is more insufferable than usual now that she's bagged herself a fellow."

"Oh, wait till you see his fake hairpiece, Barry. It's something else."

"I must pop round for a look-see."

"You can do better than that. Join us at the taverna this evening," I invited.

"What do you think, Ana?" Barry asked the baby. "Do you fancy an evening being spoiled by your Aunty Marigold and Aunty Dina?"

Little Anastasia replied in the affirmative, at least if blowing bubbles can be interpreted as a yes.

Arriving at the taverna before Marigold and our houseguests, we joined Nikos, Spiros and Vangelis at a table. Since it was too early for Nikos to light the grill, we had the pleasure of his company for a while. Dina descended and swept Anastasia away, plopping her down next to her granddaughter, Nikoleta. The toddler was quite entranced by the baby, a good sign because Nikos and Dina were eager for Eleni to produce a grandson, so eager in fact that they nagged the poor woman incessantly. Considering that Kostis was up to his old tricks of disappearing for days at a time, their nagging proved a spectacular flop on the pregnancy front.

The five of us were rather taken aback to see Guzim approach the taverna: surely he ought to be at home in the pink palace love shack making the most of his time with his young wife. Rather than entering the taverna, Guzim loitered on the doorstep, looking decidedly shifty as well as shabby. Since he made no move to shift from the entrance, Nikos went over to find out what he wanted. Watching closely, I noticed Nikos' handsome face adopt a worried expression before he called out for Vangelis and Spiros to join them. Considering that Guzim lives in the shed at the bottom of *my* garden and is in *my* employ as *my* gardener, I felt a tad put out to be excluded from what appeared to be a seriously earnest conversation. Moreover, as they insisted in speaking in muttered voices, I found it quite impossible to eavesdrop. My curiosity was piqued, to say the least.

After about ten minutes, Spiros returned to the table. Grabbing the keys to the hearse, he announced, "I must to go, the Guzim need the help." It crossed my mind that something dreadful might have happened to one of my chickens and Guzim, too embarrassed to tell me, had roped Spiros in to help him conceal the evidence.

When Spiros hurried off with Guzim, Nikos and Vangelis re-joined us. Barry didn't bother to stand on ceremony, immediately demanding, "What's going on?"

"The bad business," Nikos sighed in a heavy tone.

"The very bad business," Vangelis parroted.

"The very terrible bad business," Nikos added, determined to outdo Vangelis in the gloom stakes.

"Where has Spiros gone with Guzim?" Barry persisted.

"To the coast. They must to try to get the information from the Albanians that to work for the Besnik. The Guzim have been to the house of the foreman and it is the empty...the Besnik is the gone." Vangelis said.

"I don't understand why Spiros needs to get involved just because Besnik isn't at home," I said, rather baffled by the turn of the conversation.

"Not just the not at home. The gone. The disappeared," Vangelis stressed.

"It is the very bad," Nikos said, his eyes hooded with worry. "The word is the Besnik has to done the runner because the police are to closing in on him for the smuggling weapons."

"Smuggling weapons! Get a grip," Barry scoffed. "It sounds a bit far-fetched for anything like that to be going on round here."

Leaning forward, Nikos lowered his voice to a hiss, a rather dramatic precaution considering there was no one but us in the taverna. "*I Alvaniki Mafia* have the long reach..."

"The Albanian Mafia," Barry spluttered in disbelief.

"I've only met Besnik a handful of times but he always struck me as the decent, hard-working type…surely he wouldn't be involved with any nefarious types…"

I stopped mid-sentence, recalling that it had indeed struck me as more than a tad peculiar that Besnik was transporting rabbits over the Albanian border when he drove Luljeta to Greece. Luljeta didn't have any legal papers to enter the country and I began to suspect that perhaps Luljeta may not have been alone in her failure to be in possession of lawful documentation. Although rabbits do not require a passport to cross the border, they would certainly need to carry a certificate of health produced by a veterinarian. Perchance if Besnik had smuggled Luljeta over illicitly, he had done the same with the rabbits. And it had certainly sounded fishy when Luljeta had confided that if they were stopped, Besnik had instructed her to say that he was her husband. If Besnik had been transporting an illicit cargo of rabbits which he had exchanged for a car once over the border, was it really stretching the imagination to suppose that illegal weapons had been planted in amidst the furry cargo?

"Victor, you not to understand the way the

Alvaniki Mafia to work," Vangelis said. "They have the long tentacle; they can to force the honest man to do the dishonest work by putting the threat on the family."

"So you're saying they can force unwilling people to break the law by threatening their family members," I gasped.

"That is what I to say exactly," Vangelis confirmed.

"It is the very bad business, the dangerous," Nikos added.

"Do you all realise that Besnik drove Guzim's wife Luljeta to Greece with a truck full of rabbits?"

Nikos and Vangelis exchanged knowing looks.

"Perhaps the Mafia have to move on from the cow to the rabbit," Vangelis said.

"What?" Barry was still confused.

"They have to been smuggling the AK47s in the truck with the cow," Vangelis elaborated. "I read about it in the *To Vima*."

"The talk we hear might be the wrong," Nikos suggested. "Perhaps it is not the weapons he smuggle. The *Alvaniki Mafia* are the involve with the human organ and the narcotic too."

"It would be unhygienic to say the least to

transport human organs with rabbits," I pointed out. "Rabbits are carriers of all types of diseases that may have an adverse effect on a successful transplant. They'd need to consider the possibility of pseudotuberculosis and salmonella. I don't think humans can contract myxomatosis but…"

"Victor, have you heard yourself?" Barry shouted. "Never mind chuntering on about picking up diseases, just consider the horror of human organs being sold on the black market."

"Sorry. I got a bit carried away."

"Whatever they smuggle, the wife of the Guzim could be the cover to make all look the innocent," Nikos hypothesised.

"Do you think that they threatened her?" I couldn't believe that Luljeta was knowingly involved in criminal activity.

"She may to be the innocent dop…" Nikos struggled to come up with the English word before exclaiming, "The dope, the innocent dope…" "Dupe," I corrected. "I would stake my reputation on Luljeta's innocence. The whole thing is despicable. How could they risk such a young woman, the mother of five children, being caught up in something so abominable?"

"They not to care who the life they ruin,

they think only of money," Vangelis flatly stated. "The good thing is if the Besnik has to done the runner, he not to involve the innocent wife of Guzim any the more."

"But he was supposed to drive her home. If he has done a runner it leaves her stranded in Greece with no papers, separated from the children she adores," I cried in horror.

"We may be to jump the gun," Nikos warned. "It may not to be the true."

"But you don't believe that? That it isn't true."

"No, Victor, I not to believe that. I think the Besnik has fallen into the grip of the smuggler Mafia and used the wife of the Guzim for the cover."

"This is all such a shock. I had no idea things like this went on in Greece," Barry squealed.

"Barry, there is no the danger to you the English, trust me," Vangelis assured him, having picked up on the fear in his voice. "The *Alvaniki Mafia* threaten the other *Alvaniki*, they not to involve the foreign, not even the Greek."

"The Spiros will to sort it. The Spiros is the good man in the crisis," Nikos said. "Ah, here is the Marigold and the friend. We must not to speak again about this matter until the Spiros return. It is too much the worry for the ear of the woman."

When Nikos said that Marigold and her friend were here, I had expected to see Marigold in the company of Geraldine. Instead, I was surprised to see my wife enter the taverna arm in arm with Luljeta, although Luljeta looked quite different than she had on the first occasion I met her. As I took in Luljeta's transformation, it began to make sense why Marigold had been so desperate to shoo me out of the house earlier. She had been planning to give the young Albanian woman a makeover against my specific advice to not interfere. I had made it clear that I felt it unfair to raise Luljeta's expectations about acquiring nice things like new frocks and lippy when the Albanian couple clearly couldn't afford to indulge in such luxuries.

Fortunately, Luljeta's makeover was not as drastic as the one that Marigold had inflicted on Guzim's shed; the young woman was still as least recognisable. Gone was the shabby cotton dress that had hung on her thin frame, replaced with one of Marigold's old dresses. In truth, Marigold's style may be a touch too mature for a woman barely out of her teens, but the neat blue and white polka dot dress with its cinched waistline and flared A-line skirt suited Luljeta, giving her the air of a young housewife. I recalled that Marigold used to be very fond of that particular dress until she thickened just a tad around the waist; I have warned her about over indulging on sweet *halva* but her sweet tooth can't resist. In addition to the dress, Marigold had applied a touch of blush to Luljeta's pale cheeks and a dash of a pale lipstick, nothing too siren, to her lips. I realised that I should have trusted my wife's instincts. Luljeta remained the picture of an innocent young woman, though not quite as drab as before the makeover.

"Hello everyone, this is Luljeta, Guzim's wife. I insisted she join us. Guzim had to dash off on a job and it's no fun being stuck in a shed all alone."

Luljeta smiled shyly as she took a seat at the table. It was clear from her composure that Guzim must have protected her from the news of what was going on with Besnik. If she was in the know, I'm sure she would be a bag of nerves. Nikos excused himself to go off and light the grill. Barry asked Luljeta if she would like to meet his baby daughter and Luljeta's eyes lit up with joy. The moment she left the table, Marigold hissed in my ear, "Guzim came round in a bit of a state, quite desperate. He begged me to keep an eye on Luljeta while he went off somewhere, he wouldn't say where or why. Is there something going on that I'm not aware of?"

"There may be a bit of a problem with Luljeta not having any papers. Spiros is giving Guzim a hand to sort things out," I said, being deliberately selective with the truth. There was no point in upsetting the two women if it wasn't necessary. I dreaded to think how Marigold might react if she got wind that the Albanian Mafia may be involved.

"Where are Geraldine and Ashley? I thought he was keen to eat Nikos' organic fare?" I said.

"They'll join us a little later, dear. Earlier, when Ashley got back, he came over all mushy and said that he wished to speak privately to Geraldine. I wanted to give them some privacy to have a heart-to- heart so I sent them up to the roof terrace."

"I hope that you gave Ashley some Marmite to rub into his exposed bits. He was bitten something terrible last night," I said.

"I thought that you would revel in the idea of him scratching a nasty rash," Marigold gigled.

"Not at all," I huffed. "In fact I think we may have misjudged him."

"I was hoping you'd say that because Geraldine is awfully keen on him. If only he'd stop playing hot and cold."

"I have a feeling he's going to be pleasantly balmy this evening," I said just as Dina swooped down with the cheese and salad.

Chapter 26

Good and Kind Men

As the evening wore on, I was relieved that we hadn't shared our concerns about Besnik with the ladies: there was no point in all of us worrying unnecessarily. Along with Barry, Vangelis, and Nikos, I was more than a tad uneasy, wondering if Spiros would discover that the terrible things we had speculated about may turn out to be true. It would leave Luljeta in the most awkward position, separated from her children, effectively stranded in Greece with no legal papers or the means to return to her home in Albania. Being stuck in the pink palace of love with Guzim, seemed like little consolation.

Despite our disquietude, we were able to put on a good front. Naturally the fabulous food helped. Dina piled the table high with home-made bread and olive oil, *feta* cheese swimming in olive oil, and the freshest salad rich with the plumpest, juiciest tomatoes. A huge batch of Dina's famous chips accompanied the platter of goat chops which Nikos grilled to perfection and seasoned with garlic and oregano. When Athena telephoned Vangelis to call him home, he fobbed her off: he wanted to hang around in case he was needed on Spiros' return. I was glad that he stayed on as he is always excellent com-pany, not to mention a calming presence in a cri-sis. Marigold fussed over Luljeta like a mother hen, keen that the younger woman should enjoy the evening. In turn, Luljeta raved about how wonderful the taverna was, how modern and comfortable. Eating out was clearly a bit of a novelty if she considered the dated spit and sawdust establishment to be the height of con-temporary dining style.

As I took my turn carrying Anastasia around in my arms to rock her to sleep, Nikos approached me with a quizzical look on his face. "There is something the different about you tonight, Victor, but I cannot to put the finger on it. Ah, I have it. You have to been to the Apostolos for the cut hair."

"Do I look like I've got a lopsided neckline?" I retorted. Really, I don't know why I went to such efforts to dress more stylishly when no one in the place even noticed I'd bothered.

Handing the baby over to Marigold, she nudged me, "This is a turn up for the books, Victor. Look."

I do believe that I was less surprised than Marigold to see Geraldine and Ashley approaching the taverna together, Ashley's arm wrapped protectively around Geraldine's waist. Before they entered, Ashley drew her to him and they shared a long and lingering kiss. It seemed that Ashley was most definitely human after all, even if his hair was actually nylon.

"Their heart-to-heart must have gone well," Marigold whispered, beaming fondly at the couple as though it was she rather than me that had played the crucial role in their finally getting it together.

Considering the way that Ashley tucked

into the goat with gusto, I felt rather foolish that we had gone to such lengths to pass off the previous evening's rabbit as chicken. When it came to excellent organic fare it was those with squeamish taste buds that missed out. Thinking of the *kouneli stifado* we had dined on, I couldn't help wondering what fate awaited the truck load of likely decoy bunnies. I doubted the Albanian Mafia operated along the lines of get a free rabbit with every purchase of an AK47: I certainly hoped they didn't, otherwise the rabbits may well end up being used for target practice.

"This goat is splendid, Victor. I shall certainly listen to you when you recommend places to eat. I suppose you're up on all the best spots in Manchester with you having been a public health inspector," Ashley said.

"Victor was always reluctant to eat out back in Manchester, he was too familiar with what went on in the kitchens," Marigold laughed. "He's had to learn to be less circumspect over here…"

"I always enjoyed dining at the Bhilai Bhaji, an Indian restaurant with wonderful cuisine," I interrupted before Marigold could portray me as some stuffy type too unadventurous to eat out. "A very clean establishment scoring top marks in all areas of hygienic compliance."

"And don't forget they did the most piquant sour lemon pickle," Marigold gushed. "It seems ages since we had a good curry, Victor."

"I will cook one this weekend and utilise our very own lemons from the garden to try and replicate their pickle," I promised.

"You almost sounded homesick there, Marigold," Barry teased.

"Nonsense, Meli is home now, not Manchester. It's just a pity that the Bhilai Bhaji doesn't deliver over here."

"You could always ask Violet Burke to pick up a curry and smuggle it over in her case the next time she comes out," Barry laughed.

"I doubt there'd be any room between the smuggled Warrington eggs and the mushy peas," Marigold chuckled.

"We must have a night out at the Bhilai Bhaji when you come over to stay with me, Marigold. It will be just like old times," Geraldine gushed. Catching my eye, she clapped her hand over her mouth; it was too late, she had already put her foot in it. "You have told Victor about your plans to visit me in Manchester before Christmas?"

"No, I haven't had chance to mention it yet," Marigold blushed. "Nothing concrete, darling, just an idea. You'd manage without me for a week, wouldn't you?"

"It's no skin off my nose if you choose to go gallivanting about Manchester with Geraldine..."

"Oh Victor, I do believe you'd miss me. Nothing's settled yet but I could do the Christmas shopping. Most likely by the time I go, your mother will be over here to keep you company."

A man with a less magnanimous nature may have been inclined to sulk when such a bombshell was dropped, but I have never been one to get into a strop. I simply consoled myself with the thought that absence makes the heart grow fonder and that Marigold's excursion back to Manchester would give her the opportunity to stock up on Tesco silver skin pickles. We were running perilously low.

The table was littered with the detritus of our meal by the time that Spiros and Guzim finally returned. Once again the two men stepped outside with Vangelis and Nikos, excluding me and Barry from their confab for a second time. Now that I had an idea of what was going on, I was relieved to be left out. I had no desire to get involved with anything Mafia related. I remained close-lipped when Guzim stepped indoors, whispering something to Luljeta. The young woman's face betrayed the anxiety she bravely tried to hide as she wished us all good night, thanking us for a pleasant evening. I was touched when she turned back before reaching the door; throwing her arms round Marigold, she thanked her for all her kindness. Nikos rushed into the kitchen to speak quietly with Dina. She listened to him intently before embracing him tenderly as though sending him off on a mission. Following their short exchange, Nikos disappeared into the darkness after Spiros and the Albanian couple.

Only Vangelis returned, asking Barry and me to step outside for a quiet word. Perching on the wall, Vangelis lit a cigarette before saying, "It is true. The Besnik used the Guzim wife to make him look the more innocent when he to smuggle the weapons over the border with the rabbits. Now the Besnik is the gone and the police to want him."

"But they have no idea that Luljeta was innocently involved?"

"No, the Guzim wife is safe. Well safe, but no paper. Spiros decide the best solution is to drive the Guzim wife back to *Alvania*. The border guard not to be the suspicious of the Greek in the hearse. If there is the word of the trouble, the Guzim wife can pass the border in the coffin, they will not to check the coffin going into *Alvania*. The Mafia to smuggle into the Greece, not the other way."

"But it's such a long drive for Spiros..." Barry said.

"The Nikos go with him. The two strong men to look after the young woman. We all feel the sorry she was dragged into this, the best thing is to just get her out of the *Ellada*. If the Besnik ever to show the face round here again he will have the many angry men to answer to," Vangelis said.

"Spiros is something, isn't he, Victor. Imagine stepping in to help Guzim out like that..." Barry said.

"It will to help the Guzim yes, but the first thought was to help the young mother who was the innocent prawn," Vangelis stated emphatically.

"Pawn," I automatically corrected.

"Spiros should have said what he was planning. We could have helped out with the driving, couldn't we Barry."

"I think that would not be the good, Victor. You are helping the village by running the shop tomorrow, yes," Vangelis said. "And Barry has the baby of his own to think of...and he could never to drive so far with his terrible travel sickness."

"I suppose you're right," I agreed. Although it may not be very gallant of me to admit it, I was relieved that we had not become embroiled in such dangerous matters. I had to take my hat off to Spiros and Nikos though for the way they stepped up to help out when the cards were down, even though it didn't affect either of them personally. It made me feel immensely proud to have two such good and kind men in my corner.

"We'd better be getting home," Barry said. "I'll go in and round up the others."

Alone with Vangelis, the builder stared at me keenly.

"Victor, there is something the different about you tonight, but I not to put my finger on it." Studying me closely from head to toe, he exclaimed, "I see it. You have not to wear the ridiculous sock with the sandal."

Clapping him on the shoulder, I said, "I have to say Vangeli, you have made my evening. You're the only one who noticed."

Chapter 27

Greek Taste Buds

For the second time in a week, I woke to discover an empty space beside me in the bed. It appeared that my wife was in danger of breaking the habit of a lifetime by rising before me. I was even more surprised when Marigold appeared fully dressed, bringing me a cup of freshly brewed coffee in bed.

"Good morning, darling. What have I done to deserve such an unexpected treat?"

"Not a thing, Victor. I was so excited that I couldn't sleep."

"Thoughts of your holiday in Manchester, no doubt."

"No, nothing is even decided yet. When I got up in the night to use the bathroom, I noticed the door to your office was open and..." Marigold paused for dramatic effect..."There was no sign of Ashley on the sofa bed."

"And that filled you with excitement?"

"Must you be so dense, Victor? It means that Ashley must have spent the night in the guest bedroom with Geraldine. I expect that I will need to buy a new hat."

Marigold's good mood could not be quashed; she was fully convinced that she'd done something to inject the spark of romance into the faltering relationship of our house-guests. As I hurried to ready myself for my first day of managing the shop, Marigold hovered, insisting that she would walk me to work.

"I'll feel awkward if I'm hanging around like a gooseberry when they get up. It might embarrass them to know that I know what they've been getting up to."

"What you think you know, you know," I quibbled, convinced she was right. Obviously, Ashley had experienced a personal epiphany after confiding in me and taking my advice.

Perhaps I could offer a side-line in marriage guidance to complement my cookery classes. Norman would surely value my advice on how to adjust to Greek life without turning to the bottle or battering Doreen with a traffic cone.

"It's another beautiful day," Marigold trilled as we stepped outside arm in arm. "It's a pity you have to work, dear."

"I'm sure my wages will come in handy for that new hat you fancy."

In truth, I was looking forward to playing my part in the community by keeping the shop open in Tina's absence: after all, along with the taverna and the church, the shop was the heart of the village. The prospect of spending my day behind the till was infinitely preferable to being stuck with Geraldine and Ashley. Much as I was delighted that they had overcome their problems, I had no desire to spend the day dodging talk about VD.

I supposed that if Marigold's instinct was correct and the couple married, I would need to suffer them as holidaying houseguests for the foreseeable. It may well be in my best interest to research interesting destinations with moulage on tap in order to avoid the couple choosing to honeymoon in our guest bedroom. It struck me that practically the only downside to up-sticking to Greece was putting up with occasional company from England bedding down in our spare room. Still, once the *apothiki* was finished, we could perhaps stash any unwanted visitors down there if Violet Burke wasn't in residence.

As we passed the church, I noticed Papas Andreas loitering in the vestibule. I rather imagined that if he was waiting for Geraldine to put in an appearance, he would be sorely disappointed. I would have a quiet word with him later and assure him that Geraldine was actually in good hands; I knew that Andreas wished the best for her. I reflected that it was quite remarkable the way that the lives of our family and friends back in England were gradually becoming entwined with the lives of our friends and neighbours in Meli, the cultural and linguistic differences no barrier to developing a lasting rapport.

A small worry had been niggling away at the back of my mind ever since the mention of Marigold's trip back to Manchester. What if my wife was seduced by the life back in England and began to hanker after a reverse emigration? Naturally my heart dictated that my place was beside Marigold, wherever that may be, but I could not bear the thought of being uprooted from Greece, the country I had given my soul to.

With only five minutes to spare before I needed to open the shop, I decided to do something daring and embrace Greek time: it wouldn't do to set a precedent by actually opening on the dot. Ducking under a plane tree, I took Marigold's hand, leading her along to the edge of the square. The vantage point offered the most spectacular view, the panoramic vista of olive terraces inclining towards the sea on the horizon bathed in the early morning sunlight.

As if reading my mind, Marigold said, "You mustn't be such a worrywart, Victor. Our life is here now and I have no intention of ever returning to England except for a fleeting visit. You'll be happy enough when I return with a suitcase full of the finest pickles from Tesco."

"I don't suppose you'd throw in a few tins of Fray Bentos?"

"Really, Victor. I thought your taste buds had turned Greek."

"Oh, they have. I have something else in mind for the tinned pies rather than actually eating them," I said enigmatically.

My thoughts were already turning to my plans for the winter ahead. If Norman proved as inept as I suspected he would in getting to grips with my cookery lessons, I could always send him home with a Fray Bentos as a consolation prize.

A Note from Victor

All Amazon reviews gratefully received, even a word or two is most welcome.

Please feel free to drop me a line if you would like information on the release date of future volumes in the Bucket to Greece series at vdbucket@gmail.com

Printed in Great Britain
by Amazon